KT-562-593

Stop THE ANGER Now

A Workbook for the Prevention, Containment, and Resolution of Anger

RON POTTER-EFRON, M.S.W., PH.D

New Harbinger Publications, Inc.

Publisher's Note

This publication is designed to provide accurate and authoritative information in regard to the subject matter covered. It is sold with the understanding that the publisher is not engaged in rendering psychological, financial, legal, or other professional services. If expert assistance or counseling is needed, the services of a competent professional should be sought.

Distributed in Canada by Raincoast Books

Copyright © 2001 by Ron Potter-Efron and First Things First, Ltd.
New Harbinger Publications, Inc.
5674 Shattuck Avenue
Oakland, CA 94609

Cover design by Blue Designs
Cover image by Mel Curtis/PhotoDisc
Edited by Brady Kahn

Library of Congress Number: 01-132286

ISBN-10 1-57224-257-4
ISBN-13 978-1-57224-257-9

All Rights Reserved

Printed in the United States of America

New Harbinger Publications' website address: www.newharbinger.com

11   10   09

20   19   18   17   16   15   14

Contents

PART II
Containment

CHAPTER 8 **Containment: Spirit**   **79**

PART III
Resolution

CHAPTER 9 **Resolution: Actions**   **95**

CHAPTER 10 **Resolution: Thoughts**   **109**

CHAPTER 11 **Resolution: Feelings**   **119**

CHAPTER 12 **Resolution: Spirit**   **131**

Afterword   **147**

Getting Started

This workbook is for anyone who wants to learn some really good ways to deal with anger. Primarily though, it is designed to help people who get angry too often, become too strongly angry when they are upset, lose control of their anger, or can't let go of their anger once a situation is resolved. There is a good side to anger. It is, after all, a natural part of us. We are born with the ability to get mad. Anger has two main values. First, feeling angry tells you that something is wrong. Secondly, anger provides motivation; it gives you enough energy to do something.

But anger can become a problem. For instance, you might get angry too often. Or maybe you get so angry that you shout obscenities and become violent. Or perhaps you can't let go of your anger even after the problem is over. You can hurt a lot of people when you lose control of your anger, including yourself.

There are exactly forty-eight exercises in this workbook. That number is not an accident. Here's how they were developed.

First, anger management can be divided into three main areas: prevention, containment, and resolution. Anger *prevention* means learning ways to not get angry even when you could get angry. The beauty of prevention is that you don't waste time on useless fights. For example, it doesn't make sense to yell and scream about it getting cold in winter. Fact is, it's going to get cold whether you yell or not, so you might as well save your breath. The simple reality is that people get awfully angry a lot of times when they could relax and enjoy life instead. Anger prevention helps you decide to pass by your anger when getting angry would cause more problems than it would solve.

Next comes anger *containment*. The goal here is to keep control of your anger. It's important to stay in control because anger is a strong emotion. Anger gets intense. Just think of some of the phrases that go with extreme anger: blowing up, seeing red, going ballistic, a blind rage. Anger needs a strong container to keep it from destroying things. If you don't want to lose your health, spouse, mind, friends, job, or even your freedom, then you better learn how to keep your anger in check.

The third goal is *resolution*. Anger tells you that there's a problem. Trouble is, anger alone doesn't tell you how to solve problems. It's all too easy to waste your anger in screaming your head off. To use your anger well, you'll need to learn effective conflict-resolution skills.

So, now we have three main areas to work with: prevention, containment, and resolution. But there's another good way to divide up the anger pie. That approach is to look at four areas of change: your *actions, thoughts, feelings,* and *spirit* (this last is the big picture: the meaning of your life). For instance, maybe you got angry recently because your friend showed up fifteen minutes late for lunch. Before, you would have gone ballistic. Your actions: pointing at your watch and demanding to know why your friend was late. Your thoughts: "Some friend. He's coming late just to piss me off." Your feelings: a flushed face rage. Your spirit: "I can't trust anyone, not even my friends."

But you can change all that if you want to. New action: explain without yelling that you want your friend to meet you on time. Order ahead if you're getting hungry. New thought: "Anyone can be late once in a while. Don't make a big deal out of it." New feelings: take a few deep breaths; relax. New spirit: Give people a break. Look for what they do right instead of what they do wrong.

Three areas: prevention, containment, resolution. Four ways to change: actions, thoughts, feelings, spirit. Three times four makes twelve. Quadruple that so you have four exercises in each possible area and you end up with forty-eight exercises. Four exercises for prevention-behavior change; four for containment-thought change; four for resolution-feelings change, and so on. Forty-eight exercises that cover the entire range of anger management.

Please take your time doing these exercises. No need to rush. But it is important to do all the exercises, so you'll get a look at all forty-eight ways to deal with your anger.

Please note: I highly recommend that you read one or more of my books on anger (also published by New Harbinger Publications) as you do these exercises. The books have more general information in them as well as additional exercises. They are: *Angry All the Time, Letting Go of Anger,* and *Working Anger.* Also, if you suspect that your anger may be connected to problems with shame or low self-esteem, I suggest you read *The Secret Message of Shame,* which includes a special chapter on the shame-rage connection.

The goal is to learn how to use your anger well. If you succeed, you will be in charge of your anger instead of letting your anger control you.

PART I

Prevention

Anger is a difficult emotion to control once it gets started. Stopping your anger is like trying to catch a boulder as it bounces downhill.

So doesn't it seem like a good idea to you to keep that boulder from falling if you can? That's the idea of anger prevention: Find ways to keep from getting unnecessarily angry and you will save yourself a ton of grief.

Does this motto make sense? "Nine out of ten crises aren't!"

People are experts at creating unnecessary problems and crises. They routinely say to themselves, "What will I do if . . . ?" Or, "Boy, will I get pissed if . . ."

This kind of mental preparation—planning for the worst—may help you survive some difficult situations. But it often means you are setting yourself up to be angry when there is no real reason to get upset. The first section of the workbook is designed to help you sort out the real crises from the phony ones.

CHAPTER 1

Prevention: Actions

Exercise 1A: Choices

Getting angry is a choice. Your choice. But one thing is obvious: people who have problems with anger decide to get angry a lot more often than others. They frequently get angry about stuff they could choose to ignore. I'm not saying that it's never okay to get mad, though. There are times when anger makes sense. Getting angry is okay when:

1. somebody is doing something you really don't like, *and*

2. it's having a strong effect upon you, *and*

3. the other person can actually change their behavior, *and*

4. you have a right to get involved.

Here are a couple of examples of times when it's reasonable and fair to get angry:

You're at a campground and the people at the next site are playing loud music late at night. You don't like it, you can't sleep, they could turn the music down, and you have a right to a quiet campsite.

Your partner promises to pick you up at the mall at 5:00 P.M. but doesn't show up or leave a message. You are stranded and have to ask a stranger for a ride home. You sure don't like your partner's behavior, and it puts you in a bad situation. Your partner could have been there, and you have a right to expect people to keep their promises. Note, though, that there may be a reasonable explanation. Maybe your partner is stuck with a broken-down car and no way to contact you.

Here's the main point: *Always remember that you have a choice.* You can get angry, *or* you can choose not to get angry.

Write down here a few details about the last time you got angry—when you made a choice to get mad.

Briefly, what happened? _____

_____

When did you start getting upset? _____

_____

What did you say? _____

_____

What did you think? _____

What did you feel? _____

_____

What did you do? _____

_____

How did it end? _____

_____

Did the situation meet the four standards for when it's okay to get angry?

- Was it something you really didn't like? _____

- Did it have a strong impact on you? _____

- Could the other person have done things differently? _____

- Was it actually any of your business? _____

It's a *poor choice* to get angry when:

- It's really none of your business.

- The situation is something unimportant.

- It's about something you can't change.

- You could handle the problem just as well without getting angry.

- You hurt or scare people with your anger.

- You will get in trouble if you get mad.

- You'll do more harm than good by getting upset.

- The answer to the question, "Is this really helping the situation?" is "No."

When's the last time you made a poor choice to get angry?

- What happened? _____

- Why was it a bad choice? _____

When are you most likely to make unwise choices to get angry? In what kinds of specific situations do you get angry without a good reason? _____

Is there anything going on in your life right now that you could decide to get angry about?

_____ No

_____ Yes. If yes, what? _____

_____

What do you think you will decide? _____

_____

Why? _____

_____

Exercise 1B: The Substitution Principle: Exchanging Old Behavior for New

I'm a counselor in Eau Claire, Wisconsin. My specialty is anger management. That means I see people every day with significant anger problems. When I ask them their goal they usually say this: "I want to be less angry" or "I want to quit getting so mad all the time." Now, that definitely sounds like a goal. But it's really not. It's only half a goal. There's something important missing. What do you think it is?

The answer is that there is no mention yet of a positive goal. What is going to replace those old habits of angry actions, thoughts, and feelings?

You can't just not do things in life. You're doing something every minute you're alive. Similarly, you can't just be not angry. You have to be doing something. And, hopefully, the something you're doing will have a positive effect upon your life and upon others.

This brings us to the substitution principle: *For each angry or negative action you quit doing, you must substitute one calm or positive action.*

Practically speaking, the substitution principle takes this form: "Instead of _____ , I will now _____ ."

- "Instead of swearing I will speak politely even when I'm upset."

- "Instead of calling my kids 'stupid' when they make a mistake in their homework, I will calmly help them understand what they did wrong."

- "Instead of complaining and whining when I don't get my way, I will remind myself that disappointments are a natural part of life."

- "Instead of getting drunk when I'm upset with my wife, I will talk with her about the problem."

The substitution principle looks easy. But it can be a real challenge to come up with good, positive alternatives to those old anger habits. However, it's very important to identify these new behaviors you need to make.

If you don't substitute new, calm, and positive behaviors for your old angry ones, then the old ones will eventually return.

Are you ready to identify what you most need to do? Then fill in the spaces below:

Instead of swearing, I will _____

Instead of attacking, I will _____

Instead of name-calling, I will _____

Instead of telling people what to do, I will _____

Instead of working myself into a rage, I will _____

Instead of blaming others, I will _____

Instead of looking for things to get upset about, I will _____

Instead of feeling angry so much, I will _____

Instead of _____ , I will _____

Exercise 1C: How I Piss People Off

Everybody's good at something. If you're reading this workbook, it may be because you are really great at getting people mad at you. That can be fun, but it can also get you in a lot of trouble. Besides, you might piss people off even when you don't want to.

It's important to know exactly what you say and do that is most annoying to others. One way to find out is to ask. I've left space for you to ask five people what you do that most bothers them. But it's up to you to ask them.

Ist Person/Name: _____

What do you do that makes this person mad at you? _____

_____

2nd Person/Name: _____

What do you do that makes this person mad at you? _____

_____

3rd Person/Name: _____

What do you do that makes this person mad at you? _____

_____

4th Person/Name: _____

What do you do that makes this person mad at you? _____

_____

5th Person/Name: _____

What do you do that makes this person mad at you? _____

_____

Here's a checklist of things you might be doing that piss people off. Check the ones that fit you:

_____ Swear and cuss

_____ Threaten (Do it or else)

_____ Hit, shove, pinch, poke, slap, etc.

_____ Ignore people when they try to talk to you

_____ Gossip

_____ Criticize, put people down

_____ Sneer, get sarcastic

_____ Act superior, talk down

_____ Never praise, don't appreciate others

_____ Get jealous or envious of others

_____ Look for the worst in people and events

_____ Break promises

_____ Glare or stare at people

_____ Act defiant ("You can't make me!")

_____ Make disrespectful sounds/faces (like rolling your eyes)

Are there any other things that you do that are not on the list? _____

_____

_____

So now let's go back to the idea of choices we discussed in exercise 1A. Now that you have this information about how you piss people off, what are you going to do with it? _____

_____

_____

Exercise 1D: Doing, Not Trying

How familiar does this sound? "I'm trying to quit getting so angry."

Here's the problem with that thought: All the "trying" in the world doesn't make anything change. Or, as they say in Alcoholics Anonymous, "Trying is dying."

So it won't do you much good to try to quit being angry. You've got to make a commitment to actually change your behavior. You need to start *doing* instead of trying, *succeeding* instead of failing, *keeping your promises* instead of just having good intentions, and *stopping* your angry and aggressive behaviors instead of almost stopping. Perhaps you know yourself well enough to be able to tell when you're going to "try" versus when you're going to succeed. If so, you can fill in this table. Under "Type of Behavior," in the left column, you might write "Stop swearing or yelling," "Take a time-out," "Give praise to others," "Share non-angry feelings," or any other things you need to do.

Type of Behavior	When I'm Trying	When I'm Doing
Example: Relax	I think about it, but don't relax	I take a few deep breaths

A PROMISE TO MANAGE MY ANGER

You need to make a commitment to yourself. Sign the following agreement. It is helpful to have a witness.

I, _____ , am sick and tired of "trying" to quit being so angry or aggressive. My plan from now on is to succeed in controlling my anger. No more excuses, feeling guilty and apologizing after I've said something stupid or broken promises to be nicer to the people I care about. Today I make a pledge that I will control my anger—today, tomorrow, and every day.

That doesn't mean I'll never get angry, although part of my promise is to get angry less often. It means that if and when I do get upset about something, I will act responsibly. I will *not* scream, swear, hit, push, shove, hold, threaten, verbally abuse, or shame people. I *will* keep my temper, remain polite, look for solutions to problems instead of just staying mad, and generally keep my cool. No more trying and failing. I will *do* instead of try and *succeed* instead of fail with my anger.

My name   _____ Date _____

Witnessed by _____ Date _____

CHAPTER 2

Prevention: Thoughts

Exercise 2A: Hope for the Best, but Prepare for the Worst

Meg was raised by an angry, critical father. All she remembers from her past was him telling her what she was doing wrong. Meg heard the phrase "that's not good enough" hundreds of times. She left home as soon as she could and has seldom been back.

A few weeks ago her father called. He wants her to come home for the Thanksgiving holiday. He says he really misses her. So Meg is going to give it a try. Who wouldn't want to get along with their father, she figures. She's hoping for the best. *But, and this is important, Meg is also preparing for the worst.*

Meg: Hi, Dad.

Dad: Hi, Meg. Well, I see you've gained weight.

Meg: Dad, I thought you wanted me to come home.

Dad: I did, but I never thought you'd let yourself look that bad.

Meg sees herself feeling ashamed and wanting to run away.

Meg: Dad, I've been promoted to associate partner.

Dad: Well, it took you long enough, didn't it?

Meg anticipates feeling hurt and angry while Dad turns a good thing into something bad.

Meg: Dad, can't you say anything nice to me at all?

Dad: Oh, there you go again, always whining. If that's what you're gonna do, then you might as well leave right now.

Meg pictures herself crying, stomping out of the house and vowing never to return.

Meg needs a plan. She needs to prepare herself physically and emotionally for her dad at his worst. But she doesn't want to be scared, angry, or defensive. That will only guarantee a disaster. Here's what she comes up with:

I'll start by giving Dad the benefit of the doubt. But I'll drive my own car so I can leave whenever I want to. I will expect nothing from him—not praise, love, or appreciation. If he says anything nice to me, I will wait to see if he follows that with criticism before I take it in.

If he begins to get critical, I will remind myself that it is about him and not me. That's just what he does. But I will warn him, without anger, that if he continues to be critical I will leave. Then I'll give him a few minutes to change, but I really will leave if I have to—before, not after, he gets to me.

Hope for the best, but prepare for the worst. Then you're less likely to be surprised by a sudden attack.

For what situation coming up in your near future do you need to prepare for the worst? _____

_____

_____

What could go badly? _____

_____

_____

And how can you prepare so you won't say or do something stupid if that happens? _____

_____

_____

Exercise 2B: Know Your Hot Thoughts

Hot thoughts are the ideas you think to yourself that instantly get you angry. Hot thoughts can also be called "trigger thoughts." That's because these thoughts are the triggers for the gun called anger. Think them, and *boom*, off goes the gun. They are also referred to as "automatic thoughts" because they occur so quickly in your mind. Something bad happens (or you think about what could go wrong) and there they are, making you angry.

Hot thoughts, trigger thoughts, automatic thoughts: Whatever you call them, they cause trouble. These thoughts are the junkyard dogs in your mind. They're always ready for a fight. They snarl at everything and everybody. They're fighting beasts that never get friendly. These dogs are just plain mean. You've got to keep them on a strong leash.

Hot thoughts are usually short, vague, and overgeneralized. Here are a few samples:

- "I don't take shit from nobody."

- "I can't take it anymore."

- "Nobody appreciates me."

- "You can't trust anybody"

- "I hate you."

- "You can't make me."

- "They're out to get me."

- "How dare they say (or do) that!"

- "F--- you! F--- them!"

You don't have to say these words out loud to get mad. All you have to do is think them.

Here's space for you to identify five of your hot thoughts.

- Hot thought 1: _____

- Hot thought 2: _____

- Hot thought 3: _____

- Hot thought 4: _____

- Hot thought 5: _____

New Thoughts, Cool Thoughts

Every hot thought is like a coin. Flip it over and there's a cool thought. Cool thoughts help you stay calm. They keep you sane. For example:

- Hot Thought: "I don't take shit from nobody."

- Cool thought: "I'll listen to somebody I respect."

- Hot thought: "F--- you! F--- them!"

- Cool thought: "Slow down! Stay in control."

- Hot thought: "You can't make me."

- Cool thought: "Of course you can't, but I can choose to do what you want."

Every person has their own cool thoughts. What works for me may not work for you. The test of a cool thought is simple, though. It should help you feel calm when you think it. So if the thought "Slow down! Stay in control!" doesn't calm you down, then what could you say to yourself that would?

Go back to the hot thoughts you listed above. See if you can come up with one cool thought for each.

- Hot thought 1: _____

- Cool thought 1: _____

- Hot thought 2: _____

- Cool thought 2: _____

- Hot thought 3: _____

- Cool thought 3: _____

- Hot thought 4: _____

- Cool thought 4: _____

- Hot thought 5: _____

- Cool thought 5: _____

Exercise 2C: This Is No Time to Get Wasted

Anger is a strong emotion. You need all your attention and skill to keep it from becoming overpowering. Anger is manageable only when you're able to think well. That's why you must be very careful about your use of any mood-altering substance: alcohol, prescription medications, or illegal drugs.

Many substances are associated with increased anger and aggression.

Alcohol. Gives you an excuse ("Oh, I was drunk. I didn't really mean what I said"). Alcohol lowers your inhibitions ("I get wild when I drink"). It impairs judgment. Alcohol use often triggers totally useless arguments as well as excessive violence.

Amphetamines ("Speed") and Other Stimulants. Increase agitation. Also, you may become more easily offended. Even caffeine can be a problem.

Cocaine. Increases irritability, agitation, impulsive aggression.

Anabolic Steroids. Ever hear of "'roid rage"?

Marijuana. The myth is that it makes people more mellow. But for some people it actually increases anger and especially paranoia.

Prescription Medications, Especially Painkillers. Can decrease ability to think ahead or to accurately judge what is happening. You might also have strong or unusual reactions to certain medications.

Heroin and Other Opiates. Can lead to increased violence in order to obtain drugs.

Inhalants. May cause brain damage that lowers ability to control emotions.

Here are some of the most common ways that your anger may be connected with your use of mood-altering substances. Check all that apply and write down which substance is associated with each result. Note that different substances may have different effects upon you.

Example: I often get angrier than usual when I use crank.

_____ I often get angrier than usual when I use _____ .

_____ I can become violent when I use _____ .

_____ I make poor decisions that can get me into arguments or trouble when I use _____ .

_____ I try to tell everybody what to do when I use _____ .

_____ I won't take no for an answer when I use _____ .

_____ I get jealous or paranoid when I use _____ .

_____ I only get into trouble with my anger when I use _____ .

_____ Others tell me I seem more angry when I use _____ .

_____ Mixing _____ and _____ makes me more aggressive or argumentative.

_____ I often use _____ to try to cool down.

_____ My thinking becomes more rigid than usual.

_____ I get resentful and dwell on what people have done to me when I use _____ .

_____ Another connection I notice between my anger and my use of mood-altering substances is _____ .

Quite frankly, you may have to quit completely or at least drastically cut down your use of mood-altering substances if you get angry a lot and/or your use of those substances makes things worse.

When I take an honest look at how my drinking/taking drugs affects my anger, I'd have to say that _____

_____

So here's what I better do: _____

_____

And I will get started doing that:

_____ today

_____ tomorrow

_____ next week

_____ never

Exercise 2D: Setting Small Goals for the Future

- "I just wish that for once we could have dinner without getting into fights."

- "If I could be less angry I might live longer. I might not die of a heart attack in a rage."

- "I'd like to be able to play with the kids without someone getting hurt."

- "Maybe I could sleep through the night without waking up thinking about what went wrong earlier in the day."

These are only small goals. But they are extremely important because they show you that you are getting somewhere. They are proof that life actually gets better when you control your temper and keep yourself from getting angry.

See if you can name at least one small goal in each of the following areas that apply to your life—what you think will happen as you learn to handle your anger better.

By handling my anger better, I believe my life will change in these ways. Write down how you believe your life will improve in each category.

At home:

- with my partner: _____

- with my children: _____

- with my parents: _____

- with my brothers and sisters: _____

- during meals: _____

- at bedtime: _____

- in the morning: _____

- after school: _____

At work:

- with my bosses: _____

- with my coworkers: _____

- with those I supervise: _____

At school:

- with my teachers: _____

- with my friends: _____

- with other students: _____

In public:

- when I'm driving: _____

- when I'm shopping: _____

- when I'm with my family: _____

- when dining out: _____

- at church: _____

With myself:

- my body: _____

- my mind: _____

- my spirit: _____

- my peace of mind: _____

Anything else? _____

None of these changes are guaranteed, of course. But one thing is certain: Nothing will improve unless you prevent your anger from ruling your life.

CHAPTER 3

Feelings

Exercise 3A: Where in Your Body Do You First Feel Angry?

You've probably been asked a thousand times, "What are you feeling?" But how often have you been asked this question: *"Where* are you feeling?"

"Where are you feeling?" is a reminder that emotions like anger don't just happen in your brain. They occur throughout your whole body.

One way to prevent useless anger is to notice the very first signs of anger—your slightly curled hand (that wants to become a fist), the small furrow on your forehead, those tightened neck muscles. Your body is sending you a message: "Hey, you're starting to get mad." Once you hear that message, you can decide what to do with it. You could let yourself relax, to let go of your anger.

So where on/in your body do you first feel angry? Here's a checklist to help you answer that question. On the left, check off those parts of your body where you feel anger. In the blank space on the right, describe what you feel.

_____ Top of head _____

_____ Forehead _____

_____ Eyebrows _____

_____ Eyes _____

_____ Nose _____

_____ Cheeks _____

_____ Lips/mouth _____

_____ Chin _____

_____ Neck _____

_____ Shoulders _____

_____ Back _____

_____ Chest _____

_____ Lungs/breath _____

_____ Stomach _____

_____ Groin _____

_____ Butt _____

_____ Upper arms _____

_____ Lower arms _____

_____ Hands _____

_____ Upper legs _____

_____ Knees _____

_____ Lower legs _____

_____ Feet _____

It's a lot easier to let go of anger when it's just starting. So keep paying attention to your body. Look for those early warning signs that you're getting angry. Also, relaxing those areas of your body most susceptible to anger can help you stay in control. See exercises 3C and 7B.

Exercise 3B: HALT: Hungry, Anxious, Lonely, Tired

I first heard the acronym HALT in an Alcholics Anonymous meeting. People were talking about relapse prevention. They said that they were more likely to go back to drinking and taking drugs when they let themselves get too hungry, angry, lonely, or tired.

I've only changed one item here to make HALT useful for anger prevention. The "A" becomes "anxious" instead of "angry." So if you want to keep away from anger, you'll need to halt your hunger, anxiety, loneliness, and tiredness.

HALT isn't quite as simple as it looks, though. Why?

Hunger isn't always about food. People can hunger for food, love, attention, money, fame, and so on. Whatever you hunger for the most may make you more likely to get angry when you don't get it.

So, what do you hunger for? _____

_____

Anxiety makes anger more dangerous. Combine the two and you have "scared anger," that totally trapped—back-against-the-wall, fight-for-your-life—desperate feeling. "Blind rage," the worst kind of violence, can be the result.

How and when do you mix anxiety and anger? _____

_____

_____

What happens? _____

_____

_____

Loneliness can give a person too much time to think. One danger when you're alone is that you can start thinking over and over again about how others have hurt, abandoned, and betrayed you. But dwelling on the past that way is like drinking poison one sip at a time. You're gradually killing yourself, especially your ability to enjoy life and other people. Not only that, though. The more you obsess on your injuries, the angrier you get, until you do one of two things. First, you may isolate yourself even more, following the old, "Who needs them after all the shit they've done to me?" theory of life. That theory almost guarentees you'll be even more angry and miserable tomorrow than you are today. Secondly, you may spend a lot of time plotting how you can get back at the people who've harmed you. That's not exactly a great formula for happiness, either.

What do you think about when you're alone that gets you angry? _____

_____

_____

What else could you think about? _____

_____

_____

Tired isn't only about physical fatigue. Just like hunger, the word "tired" may refer to emotional as well as physical states. You may be tired of working twelve-hour days but also of feeling unappreciated at home, responsible for too many things, helpless about something important, and so on. You may even be tired of getting angry so often, which is one good reason to be reading this workbook.

What tires you out? _____

_____

_____

How do you get angry when you're tired? _____

_____

_____

How can you get more physical and emotional rest? _____

_____

_____

Exercise 3C: Staying Calm: Preventive Relaxation Techniques

What is the opposite of anger? Happiness? Pleasure? Actually, "calmness" is the best word. Being calm, composed, relaxed, and at peace with yourself and the world. This exercise will help you stay calm at exactly those times when you would normally get mad.

In exercise 3A I mentioned that you get angry with your body, not just your mind. Muscles tighten. Eyes glare. Breathing speeds up. Adrenaline starts rushing through you as you respond to your "fight or flight" instinct. The odd thing is that you may begin to have that response long before you actually encounter any danger. First you anticipate trouble ("Man, I'll bet Pat teases me at the party tonight"). Then you prepare for war by thinking a lot about the bad things that are going to happen. In the process, your body tenses up.

You can stop yourself from getting angry by relaxing before your body tightens. It's simple. Your body can't be both relaxed and angry at the same time. For that matter, it's pretty hard to have a tensed up ready-to-fight mind while your body is relaxed and calm.

Remember this: It's easier to stay calm in the first place than it is to return to calm after you've already gotten angry.

Here's how to keep your body relaxed even in situations in which you might often get angry.

First, quit thinking about what might be getting you upset. Instead, take a few minutes to focus on calming your body. Begin by changing your breathing. Breathe in slowly. Feel your breath going deep into your lungs. Hold it there a few seconds. Then let it out nice and slow. Repeat that several times before going on. Inhale the good air around you. Then let go of any anger or tension as you exhale.

Go to your eyes. Relax the tiny muscles around your eyes. Think "soft eyes." That's what you need right now instead of the hard, glaring eyes of anger.

Now, relax your mouth and chin. Let go of any tightness there. Breathe in a couple of slow, deep breaths through your mouth.

Your neck comes next. Swing your head around a couple times—slowly—to loosen up your neck.

And now relax your shoulders and upper back muscles. Move them in big circles to get rid of the tightness.

Before going on, take about fifteen seconds just to feel your whole body relax. Let your mind continue to relax, too, as you notice yourself becoming calmer. If any angry thoughts try to sneak in, just gently imagine them floating away as if they were tied on the strings of a balloon.

Next comes your chest. Each time you take another deep breath relax your chest muscles.

Now, relax your stomach. Relaxing your stomach really helps with fear as well as anger, so let yourself feel your anxiety draining away. Let go of any knots in your stomach. Instead, replace them with feelings of peacefulness, calmness, safety, serenity.

Keep right on relaxing. Your lower back, buttocks, and groin are next. You may have stored up anger in your back, so take a little longer there to loosen it up.

Now attend to your arms and legs. One at a time, starting with your dominant arm (your right arm if you're right-handed), let each of your limbs relax. As you become more calm, you'll probably actually feel your ams and legs warm up. That's because, when you relax, the blood that has rushed to your gut flows back into your extremities.

The place to end is to return to your breathing. Relaxation always begins and ends with your breathing. Once again, take the time to breathe slowly and deeply, feeling the air going in and out of your lungs.

Reading this exercise one time is a start. But you'll need to practice, practice, practice if you really want to become more relaxed. Twice a day for about five to ten minutes will probably be enough. You might want to make an exercise tape, so you can close your eyes while you relax.

Try working on relaxing like this for one week using the schedule that you establish (below). Then decide if relaxation is something you want or need to help you manage your anger.

Relaxation Schedule

Sunday A.M. _____   Sunday P.M. _____

Monday A.M. _____   Monday P.M. _____

Tuesday A.M. _____   Tuesday P.M. _____

Wednesday A.M. _____   Wednesday P.M. _____

Thursday A.M. _____   Thursday P.M. _____

Friday A.M. _____   Friday P.M. _____

Saturday A.M. _____   Saturday P.M. _____

Exercise 3D: Who Has Been Driving Your Life—You or Your Anger?

Imagine that your life is a bus heading down the streets of your hometown. All your feelings are sitting on the seats—Sadness, Love, Fear, Gladness, Anger, Loneliness, etc.— chatting with each other, having a decent time. None of them are any more powerful than the others. Besides, you're driving the bus. You're in control of your own life.

Then suddenly there's a revolt. Your Anger stands up, flexes its muscles, and knocks you right out of the driver's seat. Then Anger orders all the other emotions off the bus. You're left as the only passenger while Anger drives the bus of your life. Watch out! Anger drives too fast and aims at every pothole. You're in for a very bumpy ride. And, remember, this is a bus. There are no safety belts to make the trip safer.

Has this been the story of your life? Has anger been driving your life? If so, now is the time to take back control. Stand up to your anger. Make it take a passenger seat. Get back in the driver's seat. Then go back and pick up your other emotions. They need you and you need them. Notice you don't have to kick anger off the bus. It has a rightful place as one of your emotions. But you must insist that anger not run your life any longer.

How much do you agree that anger has been driving your life?

_____ Not at all

_____ That used to be true but not anymore

_____ I guess you could say that some of the time

_____ Oh yeah, that's exactly my situation

In your mind what does your angry bus driver look like? _____

_____

_____

What has it felt like to be out of control of your own life? _____

_____

_____

How do you think your life would be different if you could get into and stay in the driver's seat? _____

_____

_____

How would you feel? _____

_____

_____

Who would you tell the good news to first? _____

Who else would you tell? _____

_____

How would you celebrate this important moment in your life? _____

_____

_____

What will you do if your anger gives you a hard time? What if it doesn't want to get out of the driver's seat? _____

_____

_____

What will you do if anger tries to sneak back into the driver's seat when you're not looking? _____

_____

_____

What steps have you taken, so far, to get back to the driver's seat? _____

_____

_____

What steps do you still need to take?

1. _____

   _____

   _____

2. _____

   _____

   _____

3. _____

   _____

   _____

CHAPTER 4

Prevention: Spirit

Exercise 4A: Challenging Your Angry Spirit

Looking at your spirit means attending to the bigger picture, namely the meaning of your life. What are you doing here on this planet? What are your hopes and dreams? How do you want to connect with others? How generally optimistic or pessimistic are you? Do you expect things to turn out well or poorly?

Anger has a devastating effect on the spirit. Anger that comes and goes quickly is bad enough. The real problem comes about if you are someone who gets angry a lot. You're carrying around a chronically angry spirit. That's heavy baggage to go through life with. It's bound to bog you down. Nothing much will happen—you'll never quit being angry—until you challenge and change your perpetual negativity.

The following quiz contains a list of statements. Please apply a number to each statement indicating how much you believe it to be true. Use a scale of 0 to 10, where 0 means "I don't believe that at all," and 10 means "I completely believe this is true, with no exceptions."

Be sure to give honest answers, not what you think others want you to put down.

The Angry Spirit Quiz

_____ Life sucks and then you die.

_____ People cannot be trusted.

_____ There's way more bad than good in this world.

_____ I have every right to be angry because of what I've gone through.

_____ Nothing good lasts. Something bad always ruins everything.

_____ Never forgive and never forget.

_____ People who've hurt me deserve to be punished.

_____ It's other people's fault, not mine, that I'm so angry.

_____ People who are nice to others always get hurt.

_____ People who are kind to others are fools.

_____ You can't let anybody see your real feelings.

_____ People really are out to get me.

_____ When I think about my life, I feel bitter and resentful.

Total score _____

Adding up all the items gives you your Angry Spirit score. How do you feel about it? Maybe it's time to see what you can do to reduce that score. Where do you start? That's easy. Just pick one statement from the list that you scored high on. Select one that strongly affects your life.

Which statement do you need to work on first? _____

_____

What would be the exact opposite statement? (For instance, the opposite of "Life sucks and then you die" might be "Life is good, so live it well.") _____

_____

Consider this new statement for a few minutes. How does it grab you? Could you try it out for a few days to see how well it works? Will you?

Maybe this new statement is still too strong a voice in you right now. Okay then, see if you can come up with a statement about halfway between all negative and all positive. (For instance, "Sometimes life sucks, but sometimes it's good, too.") Try that on for size. Can you live with it? Will you?

What would this new (halfway) statement be? _____

_____

Keep challenging every negative statement on which you scored high. The goal is to at least adopt a neutral attitude. That's where the world is neither good nor bad. It just is.

Exercise 4B: Accepting Reality: You Can't Always Get What You Want

Joe has a problem. He wants sex. He wants it now. His partner, Pat, isn't interested right at the moment. So Joe goes nuts. He pouts. He demands. He guilt-trips. He calls Pat names. He threatens to find someone else. Finally he stomps off.

Joe has a simple philosophy: I want what I want and I want it now! Give it to me or else. It's mine, all mine. My way or the highway. Do what I say because I'm saying it. I'm in control. Watch out, or I'll get mad.

If only the world would cooperate. Then everybody would have only one purpose in life—to serve Joe. He'd be completely in charge, not only of his life but of everyone's. He'd get whatever he wanted whenever he wanted it: food, attention, sex, power, money, drink, even love.

But, the real world doesn't work that way. As the Rolling Stones put it, "You Can't Always Get What You Want." And that's frustrating. It can be very hard to accept the idea that you are only a tiny speck in the universe and that nobody owes you anything.

But as my wife once said, "Expect a lot and you'll be frequently disappointed. Accept a lot and you'll be frequently delighted!"

A lot of useless anger is the result of unrealistic expectations. Here's what happens:

> You expect too much.
> You don't get what you want.
> You become frustrated.
> You get mad.
> You make demands.
> You still don't get what you want.
> You get more angry.
> You threaten.
> You attack.

How familiar is this pattern to you?

The best place to break this sequence is at the first step. Don't expect more than the world can deliver and you won't get so disappointed and angry.

But how can you tell if your expectations are realistic or unrealistic? Use these guidelines. An expectation of others is usually realistic if:

1. the other person can give you what you want;

2. the other person wants to give you what you want;

3. giving you what you want doesn't take away from what the other person wants or needs;

4. giving you what you want doesn't make the other person feel disrespected, ashamed, guilty, or bad.

Name three areas in your life in which you consistently expect more from others than you get?

1. _____

2. _____

3. _____

What do you think, feel, say, and do when your unrealistic expectations aren't met? _____

_____

_____

If other people haven't been put on this planet just to serve you, what are they here for? _____

_____

_____

What can you say to yourself to help you accept the fact that you can't always get what you want? _____

_____

_____

Please go back to the first set of questions. Can you think of more realistic expectations for those three areas of your life in which you consistently expect more from people than you actually get?

1. _____

2. _____

3. _____

Exercise 4C: What Would You Do If You Weren't So Angry?

What do you think of this goal: "I want to be less angry."

It's not a bad idea, is it? But still something is left out. There is no positive direction. The only desire is to do less of something. That's not enough. Doing less of something only creates a vacuum. Something has to fill that vacuum.

You need to complete this sentence: "I want to have less anger and have more . . ."

Frankly, I don't think people can stay less angry unless they become more of something else. But what that "more" is varies from person to person.

Here is a checklist of some of the most frequent positive goals you might embrace. Rank in order the ones that you want more of in your life, in which 1 is the goal you want most, 2 is second-most, and so on. Put a "0" to indicate any that you're not interested in.

Example: I want to have less anger and to have more:

__2__ serenity

__3__ fun with others

__0__ quiet times

__1__ stimulating discussions

This person most wants stimulating discussions and has very little interest in quiet times. Remember that there's a huge difference between stimulating discussions and arguments; you can have one or the other but not both. Now, your turn.

I want to have less anger and to have more . . .

_____ fun with others

_____ acceptance of others

_____ appreciation of others

_____ ability to forgive

_____ connection with God or something greater than myself

_____ a feeling of calmness and serenity

_____ stimulating discussions

_____ quiet times

_____ ability to show love and caring

_____ respect for the wants and needs of others

_____ ability to solve problems peacefully

_____ empathy (understanding how others think and feel)

_____ ability to see the good in the world

_____ productive time where I can get things done

_____ ability just to enjoy life

_____ awareness of my other feelings

If you have other goals, add them to the list.

_____

_____

_____

A Vision of a Better Future

Now that you know what you want, take a few minutes to find a comfortable place to sit or lie down. Let yourself imagine yourself doing the first few things you've checked off. If, for instance, your top goal is have more ability to show love and caring, then close your eyes and see yourself doing exactly that. Let yourself notice how good you feel when you're less angry and more loving.

This vision is vital to your future. Keep it in your memory. Return to it frequently. Let it serve as a guide to your actions, feelings, and choices.

Exercise 4D: Self-Hate: The Saboteur of Anger Management

Self-hatred is a combination of anger and shame turned inward. The anger makes people attack themselves whenever they do anything wrong or when they fail at something. The shame makes them think they will never get better. Together, anger and shame produce this thought: "I screwed up my life in the past, I'm screwing it up now, and I will certainly screw it up in the future." Self-hatred sabotages anger management for one simple reason: It's hard to treat others decently when you are being mean to yourself.

Here's a checklist of some of the things self-hating individuals think and do. How many apply to you?

_____ I get really angry at myself a lot.

_____ I often neglect my own basic needs, such as dressing appropriately, eating good food, or making doctor appointments when I'm not feeling well.

_____ I don't like almost everything about myself: the way I look, what I do, how I think, who I am.

_____ I often think one or more of these thoughts: "I'm no good"; "I'm not good enough"; "I'm unlovable"; "I don't belong"; "I should not exist."

_____ I frequently call myself nasty names like "stupid," "worthless," or "ugly."

_____ I regularly swear at myself.

_____ I look for proof that I am a bad person rather than for signs that I am good.

_____ I often want to punish myself even though I haven't done anything wrong.

_____ I ignore praise or refuse to believe it when people say nice things about me.

_____ I often fail at what I do because I expect to fail or believe I don't deserve success.

_____ I literally attack myself by punching, cutting, burning, or hurting my body in other ways.

_____ I think of myself as beyond hope. I'll never be good for anything or anyone.

_____ I often think about killing myself or wish I would die.

Are you full of self-hate? If so, you need to make and keep one promise as you read through this workbook: *I will give myself exactly the same gifts I am learning to give to others.* So, if you give others the gift of looking for the good in them, then start looking for the good in yourself as well. Or if you are giving them the gift of praise, then begin praising yourself. Give respect to others and to yourself. If you choose not to swear at them, then don't swear at yourself, either.

Remember that self-hate may sabotage your efforts to quit getting so angry with others. If you don't start treating yourself better, you probably won't be able to keep control of your anger. You'll help others by helping yourself. This is a situation where everybody can win.

Take another long look at this statement: "I will give myself exactly the same gifts I am learning to give others." Is this a promise that you are willing to make, right now, to yourself?

PART II

Containment

Everybody gets angry from time to time, but not everyone blows sky high when they do. Some people have learned how to control themselves. At the emotional level, they don't let their anger turn into rage. At the action level, they can express their anger without getting aggressive, attacking, or intimidating others. Above all, they never use the excuse that they did something harmful just because they were mad.

Imagine that you could take your temperature when you get angry. A little anger would be okay. That would be like raising your temperature a couple of degrees. But any higher and you've got a fever. That fever is a sign that something has gone wrong. You're too hot. Your blood is starting to boil and you're losing control. It's almost impossible to communicate effectively when you get that mad. Instead of dialogue, you have monologue—one person yelling at the other and not listening.

The goal in this section of the anger workbook is to help you stay in control of your anger. The idea is to contain your anger, to keep your temperature down. This isn't prevention, though. I'm not suggesting you let go of your anger completely. Just keep it in check. Don't let runaway anger destroy your life.

CHAPTER 5

Containment: Actions

Exercise 5A: Time-out: Recognize, Retreat, Relax, Return

What Is a Time-out?

A time-out is a choice you make to leave a situation before you say or do something aggressive, damaging, or hurtful. We're talking adult time-outs here, by the way. There isn't any parent telling you to go to your room; there's only you deciding that you better take a time-out before you say or do something bad. You're not running away, either. Instead, you are taking responsibility by leaving temporarily so that you can regain control of your body and mind.

Why Take a Time-out?

Taking a time-out can sometimes be your last hope, the only thing that can stop an opponent who has broken through the rest of your defenses. The opponent is your anger. If that anger turns into rage—if you start yelling, cursing, throwing, hitting—you may end up getting thrown out of the game (job, marriage, friendship) and into the penalty box (isolation, homelessness, jail).

The bottom line is this: You take a time-out to protect yourself and others from your fists and your mouth. The issue is safety.

When to Take a Time-out

You're ready to explode. You can feel it in your chest, the way it's tightening up. Your voice is rising. You're pacing around the room faster and faster. Your hands keep turning into fists. You're thinking something like, "I can't take this anymore." You're not listening to what people are saying, at least not to anything that might calm you down. Basically, you are past the point of no return. You're gonna blow—unless you *get out now.*

How do you take a time-out? Here's a simple memory aid that can help you take a good time-out: Recognize. Retreat. Relax. Return.

Recognize When You Need a Time-out

You can't take a time out if you don't realize you need one. You must recognize the signs that you are losing control. Write down five signs that let you know when you are losing control of your anger. These are things that you think, say, feel, and do right before you explode, such as clenching your jaw, raising your voice, or thinking that someone is a bitch or an asshole.

_____

_____

_____

_____

_____

Retreat

Retire. Leave. Get out. Believe me, this is no time to make one last point. You may only have thirty seconds or less before you explode. Forget your pride issues, too. Remember, you'll lose a lot more of your dignity by screaming your head off than you will by leaving before any damage is done. Don't make any of these excuses to stick around when you know you should leave:

- "I've got nowhere to go." (So go anyhow—walk around the block if you need to.)

- "Why should I have to leave? Why shouldn't he (or she)?" (We're not talking equal opportunity or long-term fairness here. The issue is safety, so get out before someone gets hurt.)

- "I'm waiting for a phone call." (If you don't get out now, the next call you'll be waiting for may be from your probation officer.)

What excuses might you make not to take a time-out when you need one?

_____

_____

Here's what to say: "I've got to take a time-out. I'm leaving right now for a while. I'll be back as soon as I can."

And then go. Go. Go. Go. Get out now.

Relax

Go somewhere and do something that helps you relax. Take a long walk. Read a book. Drink some decaffeinated coffee. Exercise. Meditate. Whatever you do, you should be able to feel the anger draining out of your system. If that isn't happening, then do something else. Try to find something you can throw yourself into, so you won't keep churning up your anger.

Don't talk with people who will only throw fuel on your fire. ("Man, did you get a raw deal. You should go back there and tell them off good.") Don't watch violent movies. Don't drink or get high. Use your head. Remember, the goal is to feel better and to let go of your anger.

Write down three things you can do when you take a time-out that will help you relax.

1. _____

2. _____

3. _____

Return

Now comes the hardest part. Going back to the scene of the fight. But that's the biggest difference between taking a time-out and running away. In a time-out, you return after you've calmed down, in order to try to resolve the problem that got you so angry in the first place. You'll need to use the conflict-management skills discussed in part III of this workbook. Make sure you've looked them over.

One more thing: Don't return expecting that the person you got so mad at will be in a good mood. Maybe he or she will. Maybe not. Be prepared to handle someone else's anger or defensiveness. Don't go back until you can keep your cool even if the other person can't.

When you return, what do you most need to remember? _____

_____

Remember the Four R's of a time-out: Recognize. Retreat. Relax. Return.

Exercise 5B: I Know Exactly How to Hurt Them, but I Won't

Certain people are special. Your partner. Your kids. Your longtime coworkers. Your friends. You know what they like. What they dislike. Their loves, their joys. And most of all, their soft spots. In other words, you know exactly what you could say that would really hurt them.

Now you're getting angry. They've disagreed with you. You're frustrated. Perhaps this is the time to whack them with a special insult that hurts them in a soft spot. Maybe: "There you go again. You're just like your father." Or "You're so lazy you make me sick." Or "You're fat and ugly." Or "You can't do anything right, can you?"

Whatever it is, you know it will work. That one statement will make the other person feel awful. True, they may retaliate by saying something equally nasty about you, but at least you'll have gotten in one strong blow. It would feel good, too. Who doesn't want to hurt people who won't do what we want?

A big part of getting control of your anger involves saying no to your own desire to attack. No thanks, I think I won't say that. I'm tempted. But I won't. I could hurt him. I could hurt her. But I choose not to.

Why not, though? Why shouldn't you go for the jugular vein? Here are several reasons to hold back. You decide which are most important to you. In the left column are a list of reasons. In the righthand column, write "none," "a little," or "a lot" to indicate how much these reasons matter to you.

Reason	Importance to You
If I do, he/she will say something hurtful back.	
Saying that will only make things worse.	
I'm trying to be more respectful of others.	
Even when I'm angry, I don't want to harm people.	
I'm getting too old for this nonsense.	
Saying mean things is sinful or morally bad.	
I don't want others to see me this way.	

I wouldn't want to be treated that way by others, so I won't do that to them.	
I don't want to destroy this relationship.	
I just don't feel good about myself when I act like that.	
I'll never gain control of my anger if I keep saying hurtful things.	

Are you willing to quit saying the harmful things that you know will hurt others? If so, make a list (in your mind or on paper) of the phrases that are especially damaging. Then make a promise to yourself that you will never say those things again, no matter how angry you get.

Exercise 5C: Do Something Different

First I said . . .
Then she said . . .
Then I said . . .
Then she said . . .

It's the same old fight in the same old way. You could say your lines in your sleep. For that matter, you could say the other person's lines in your sleep as well. I call these "Here We Go Again" arguments. Just about every group has them: couples, parents with their kids, coworkers, etc. The ways you can tell you're in a Here We Go Again argument are that:

1. Something very predictable happens. (Once again you forgot to pick up some milk for the kids.)

2. The other person complains in their usual manner. ("You forgot *again*! Boy, are you a dope.")

3. You defend yourself the same way you always defend yourself. ("I'm not a dope. It's all your fault anyhow. You know how tired I get at the end of the day. You should have gotten the milk yourself, you lazy . . .")

4. The fight goes on long enough so everybody gets really frustrated.

5. But nothing ever gets resolved.

6. So you'll have the same fight all over again in a couple more days.

Here We Go Again arguments are a huge waste of time and energy. But how can you stop them? You have two choices.

1. Don't even bother bringing up the subject.

2. Do something different when the subject is brought up.

Writing down your answers to the following questions will help you decide which tactic to try. Name two Here We Go Again fights you get into and write down the first four steps in the argument. Here's an example:

Name: The "Kids, Pick Up Your Room" Fight

1st Step: I say, "Kids, your room is a mess. Go pick it up right now."

2nd Step: They say, "Aw, Mom (Dad), let us finish this show. It will be over in a half hour."

3rd Step: I get mad and say, "You kids always say that, but then you don't clean it up. Get up there now!"

4th Step: They shout at me that I'm being mean, and they still don't go to their room.

Your turn:

Name of Here We Go Again fight: _____

1st Step: _____

2nd Step: _____

3rd Step: _____

4th Step _____

List another Here We Go Again fight:

Name of Here We Go Again fight: _____

1st Step: _____

2nd Step: _____

3rd Step: _____

4th Step _____

Now you have some choices to make. If you want to avoid another useless argument, you can simply choose not to bring up the matter. For instance, how big a deal is it if the kids' room is a mess? After all, aren't almost all kids' rooms like that? Besides, arguing with them won't get the room cleaned anyhow. It will only make you mad. So, maybe the best thing to do is to take a deep breath and put their room in the "not worth fighting about" area of your brain.

The other thing you can try is to be a little more creative. You can do something different that breaks the routine. For instance, the parent in the scene might try one of these strategies:

1. Compromise by saying, "Okay. Tell you what. I'll watch the rest of the show with you and then we'll all work on your room."

2. Offer to clean the room for a fee (to be taken out of the kids' allowances if they get one).

3. Put up a "Watch Out for Crawling Objects" sign on the door of their room for them to think about.

The idea is to try something different. Whatever it is will break the routine. You may be able to laugh instead of argue. Or perhaps now you'll find some ways to actually deal with the situation instead of just going in circles.

Now, please go back to the two Here We Go Again arguments you described. What could you do differently in each?

1st Fight:

I could _____

Or I could _____

Or maybe I could _____

2nd Fight:

I could _____

Or I could _____

Or maybe I could _____

Exercise 5D: Turning Down the Heat

- Hot
- Fuming
- Inflamed
- Flaming
- Hot under the collar
- Seething

- Boiling mad
- Fiery
- Burning up
- Hotheaded
- All hot and bothered
- Simmering

Have you ever noticed how many words and phrases describing strong anger refer to heat? I suppose that's because your blood starts circulating faster when the "flight or fight" response to perceived danger kicks in. Feeling the heat is a sure sign that you're beginning to lose control of your anger.

The goal of this exercise is to think of ways to lower the heat once the fire has been ignited, in other words, how to contain your anger even when you are angry. How can you put out the fire or at least keep it from burning everything down?

Imagine for a minute that you are the chief of fire control for about 100,000 acres of forested land in Idaho or Montana. You've just been informed that a potentially severe fire has been spotted on that land. What would you do? You could:

- Fly over the fire to observe it.

- Get people out of harm's way.

- Send in fire-fighting equipment.

- Drop water on the flames.

- Light a backfire to keep the fire from spreading.

- Make a call for more help if absolutely necessary.

Now let's make a few parallels that connect your real life with this scene:

Fire Chief	Real Life
Observes the fire.	You notice that you are getting very angry.
Makes sure nobody gets hurt.	You take a time-out if necessary.
Sends in fire-fighting equipment.	You practice exercises such as relaxation that help you contain your anger.
Drop-water on the flames.	You cool off by telling yourself to calm down.
Lights a backfire to control the fire.	You let people know you are upset and discuss your concerns instead of losing control.
Calls for help.	You talk with people who can help you calm down.

Can you think of another analogy that describes your hot anger? A bomb exploding? A hot day with storm clouds coming in fast? A keg of dynamite with a lit fuse? Sitting in a steam bath or sauna? A blast furnace? If so, fill in the blanks:

My hot anger is like a _____ .

Some ways you can control this kind of anger are:

• _____

• _____

• _____

• _____

• _____

• _____

Now let's connect again to real life.

My Analogy   **My Real Life**

_____   _____

_____   _____

_____   _____

_____   _____

_____   _____

_____   _____

CHAPTER 6

Containment: Thoughts

Exercise 6A: Don't Jump to Conclusions (Don't Get Paranoid)

Your good friend just told you that he's asking someone else to be the best man at his wedding.

You immediately think: "That jerk. He tricked me into thinking he's my best friend. I'll never trust him again."

Wait a minute, though. This guy's been your buddy for years. He's never done anything to hurt you. Why are you reacting so strongly?

Here's another scenario: Your partner is a half hour late for dinner. You immediately think: "I'll bet he's hitting on someone. He's cheating on me."

Hold on there. You've been together for over a year. As far as you know he's never cheated on you. Matter of fact, you've never even seen him flirting with anyone else. What's happening to you?

Irrational doubt. Unreasonable distrust. Excessive suspiciousness. Mindless fear. Paranoia. These thoughts and feelings set the stage for anger and aggression.

How often do you find yourself jumping to conclusions?

____ Never

____ Once in a while

____ Pretty often

____ A lot

____ All the time

It's a small step from jumping to conclusions to paranoia. Paranoia occurs when you falsely believe people want to harm you. So here is a question.

How often do people say that you are getting paranoid? That you are accusing them or others of trying to harm you when they're not? That you assume the worst about them or others?

____ Never

____ Once in a while

____ Pretty often

____ A lot

____ All the time

Low self-worth causes people to jump to the wrong conclusions and to become paranoid. If you don't like yourself much, it's easy to believe others also don't like you. It's an easy move from that thought to the belief that people are just using you for their own purposes. The next time you make this mistake, ask yourself this question: "Why am I feeling so bad about myself right now?"

Paranoia can also result from what's called projection. You think someone wants to hurt you when really it's you who wants to hurt them. So ask yourself another question the next time you get paranoid: "What am I angry at them about?"

Here are five thoughts that might help you be less paranoid. Which one will help you the most? If none of these work for you, come up with another thought that will help you trust others more.

- "Nobody's out to get me."

- "Don't assume the worst."

- "Now, don't get paranoid."

- "Give them the benefit of the doubt."

- "I choose to trust."

If this exercise strikes home, you might want to read more about paranoia. If so, you could begin by reading my chapter on paranoia in *Letting Go of Anger*.

Exercise 6B: Don't Make a Bad Situation Worse

Your twelve-year-old kid comes home shaved bald on one half of her head and with green hair on the other. She didn't ask permission. You're not happy about this. You march toward her to tell her just that. But before confronting her, remind yourself to avoid three costly mental errors. Don't awfulize, devilize, or personalize. These three mistakes all make a bad situation worse. Make them and you'll probably lose control. Here's what you might say:

- Awfulizing: "That's terrible. I can't stand it. That's the worst thing you've ever done."

- Devilizing: "You must have joined a cult."

- Personalizing: "You did do that just to hurt me, didn't you?"

Each of these mental mistakes turns your child into an enemy. She becomes a dangerous opponent whose only goal is to make your life miserable. You forget that she's really a good kid. You forget that you love her. Then you attack.

By the way, you don't need another person in the room to make these mental errors. It's all in your head, so you can be awfulizing, devilizing, and personalizing while you're driving in your car, sitting alone in your kitchen—anytime, any place. You've got to catch yourself whenever and wherever you start making these mental mistakes.

When's the last time you awfulized? _____

About what? _____

What was the result? _____

_____

Who is the last person you devilized? _____

Why? _____

What was the result? _____

_____

What's the last thing you took too personally? _____

Why do you think you reacted that way? _____

What was the result? _____

_____

    Here are some thoughts that can help you keep things in perspective. Check off the ones you most need to remember:

To prevent awfulizing:

____ This is no big deal. I can handle it.

____ On a scale of 1 to 10 how important is this?

____ This is a disappointment, not a disaster.

____ Don't make a bad situation worse.

____ Nobody died here, so it's not so awful.

To prevent devilizing:

____ Just because I don't like it doesn't make it evil.

____ He/she doesn't have horns on his/her head.

____ He/she is a good person.

____ I'm no better than anybody else.

____ Maybe my way isn't the only way.

To prevent personalizing:

____ Don't take things so personally.

____ He/she didn't do this just to hurt me.

____ It's not about me, it's about them.

____ I need to back off.

____ I don't have to take responsibility for their choices.

Exercise 6C: Disputations and Anger Control

Disputation is a thinking process that will help you stay in control of your mind while you are talking with others. It's a way to challenge the kind of thinking that only makes a bad situation worse. Getting angry is a process with several steps, and you can intervene in this process.

1. First comes the **antecedent**. Someone has done or is doing something that you might get angry about.

2. Second are your **irrational beliefs** and thoughts, convincing you that you have a right to get angry. "Irrational" here means that these beliefs exaggerate the problem, make the problem impossible to fix, or just don't make much sense to anyone but yourself.

3. The **consequences** of your irrational beliefs are: anger, hostility, and/or aggression.

4. But you don't have to get angry (step 2). Your **disputation** is a new belief or thought that is far less anger-provoking than your irrational beliefs. So you substitute this new thought for these other beliefs.

5. The positive **effects** of your new thoughts are: less anger, less hostility, less aggression.

   Here's an example:

1. Your child forgot to mention he'd be home an hour late.

2. You think: "That's awful. I can't take it. How dare he do that to me."

3. You yell at him and ground him for good.

4. New thought: "Everybody forgets once in a while. He's just a kid. No damage done. No big deal."

5. You remind your son that it's important for him to let you know when he'll be delayed.

   The key to this technique is to substitute the new thought (step 4) for the irrational beliefs (step 2). This helps you stay in control in situations where you have some reason to be upset but you don't want to blow everything way out of proportion. In other words, just because something goes wrong is no reason to go crazy.

Your turn now. Pick a time when you got way too angry about something that went wrong. Then go through the five-step process.

1. What happened? _____

_____

2. What did you believe that made the situation worse? _____

_____

3. What were the consequences of that belief (what did you do)? _____

_____

4. What could you have thought instead? _____

_____

5. What might have resulted? _____

_____

_____

What about right now? Is anything going on in your life that you have been overreacting to? If so, try another disputation. Your new thought (step 4) should make sense to you. Just as importantly, it should help you feel more calm and in control. If it doesn't, keep thinking until you come up with a new thought that really works.

Note: This exercise and exercise 2B work well together. Using both on a regular basis will help you think much more clearly in anger-provoking situations.

Exercise 6D: How Do You Justify Your Anger?

You may very well feel guilty or ashamed after you've become really angry, especially if you said or did things that harmed others or made them look foolish. But you avoid that "I sure screwed up" feeling if you point your finger at someone else and say, "It's all your fault. You're the one who screwed up, not me. I have the right to be angry because of what you did."

What a deal! It's all their fault! They're the troublemakers. You can go ahead and blast them without so much as a twinge of guilt. They deserve it because of what they did to you.

So what's the problem? Simple: As long as you blame other people for your behavior, you will never change your behavior. You'll just keep getting mad without ever noticing that you could choose to be far less angry (see exercise 1A: Choices). You'll keep demanding that others change without asking yourself how you could change.

There's another problem: When you justify your anger, you are giving yourself permission to get really angry. After all, they've done something terrible to you. Besides, it's all the other person's fault. You might as well get really angry and completely blow your top.

How do you usually justify your anger? Here's a checklist of possibilities. Before you do this exercise, though, think of a few times you have become or stayed really angry. What did you think to yourself that maintained or increased your anger? You may notice that your justifications for being angry are different with different people. That's important information if you want to blame others less and take more responsibility for your anger.

Complete the following statement. Select all the justifications that you know you've used.

I have a right to be really angry with you (or them) because:

_____ it's all your (their) fault.

_____ I'm right and you're (they're) wrong.

_____ you (they) are being unfair to me.

_____ you (they) have been so thoughtless or inconsiderate.

_____ you (they) could have prevented something bad from happening to me.

_____ you've (they've) hurt me so badly.

_____ I think you (they) hurt me on purpose.

_____ of all the mean things you've (they've) said or done to me in the past.

_____ you (they) should be punished for what you've (they've) done to me.

_____ you (they) just won't do what I want even though what I want is perfectly reasonable.

_____ you (they) are immoral, bad, evil, or stupid.

Are you ready to quit blaming others for your anger? If so, here's how.

1. Review the list above. Select one or two justifications that you use very frequently.

2. Make a personal commitment to quit thinking that way to yourself and to quit making those excuses for your anger to others.

3. If you do hear yourself justifying your anger by blaming others, make yourself stop and substitute this (or a similar) new thought: "Wait a minute. I've promised myself I won't blame others for my anger. They're not making me mad. I am."

4. Then ask yourself what is going on that is upsetting you so much. Is it that you aren't getting what you want? Or maybe that you are feeling out of control? Or that you are anxious, depressed, worried, or hurting physically? Keep the focus on you, not the other person.

5. Once you've identified what's bothering you, ask yourself what you need to do to feel better: take a time-out; relax; calmly talk with the other person; ask directly for what you want; accept reality.

6. Be sure to reward yourself whenever you've accepted responsibility for your own anger. "Hey, I did it. I didn't blame them for my anger. I took responsibility. I did it right. Good for me!"

The justifications for my anger I most need to challenge are: _____

_____

_____

CHAPTER 7

Containment: Feelings

7A: Notice Your Other Feelings

Sad	*Glad*	*Scared*	*Lonely*	*Guilty*	*Ashamed*
Anxious	*Bored*	*Tired*	*Hurt*	*Disgusted*	*Jealous*
Surprised	*Amused*	*Worried*	*Envious*	*Depressed*	*Hopeless*

Anger is a runaway emotion. Once you begin to get mad, your anger runs away from all your other feelings. You think: "I'm pissed and that's all there is to it." You probably don't think: "Well, yeah, I'm angry all right, but I'm also feeling scared and hurt." But that's exactly how you do need to think to prevent your anger from taking over. You need to keep in touch with all your other emotions.

Here's a phrase to remember: *Anger can be a cover emotion.* This means anger can feel so powerful it hides all your other feelings. Imagine your anger is a blanket hiding all your other feelings beneath it. You won't know what they are until you peek under that blanket.

Here's another phrase to remember: *Anger seldom rides alone.* This means when something happens that is strong enough to trigger your anger, chances are it also triggers other feelings.

Imagine the following situations. Ask yourself what other feelings you would have in addition to anger in each.

- You're walking down the street and a car racing by almost hits you. If that happened I would probably feel anger and _____.

- Your best friend tells you he or she recently had sex with your partner. If that happened I would probably feel anger and _____.

- Someone stole your wallet and now you don't have enough money to buy food for your family. If that happened I would probably feel anger and _____.

- Your teacher or supervisor criticizes your work in front of your group. If that happened I would probably feel anger and _____.

- What other feelings are you most likely to have when you get mad?

  _____

  _____

- What other feelings are you most likely to ignore? _____.

  _____

  _____

So now what? Here's what you can do with those other feelings that will help you control your anger

1. Identify them. ("I'm angry, but I'm also _____.")

2. Mention them. ("George, I'm mad at you for forgetting our date. But I also feel insecure because I'm not sure I matter to you.")

3. Focus on each feeling and what you want or need. ("George, I want an apology but I also need some reassurance that I'm important to you.")

4. You may have to deal with each feeling separately. Don't let yourself focus exclusively upon your anger.

   Ignoring those other feelings is a big mistake. Don't make it.

Exercise 7B: How to Relax in the Middle of an Argument: A Pocket Guide

I first described relaxation techniques in exercise 3C. Those techniques are most useful to prevent you from getting upset in the first place. But what if you are in the middle of a discussion with someone and you can feel yourself tightening up? Your body has already begun its "fight or flight" reaction. You're going to need some quick ways to reduce your bodily levels of anger and anxiety. That's what this exercise is for.

You'll need a three-by-five-inch index card for this exercise. You can't get many words on an index card. But that's good. You need a quick guide when you're already mad. Right down some key words to remind yourself what you most need to do to relax. The best guides have no more than six brief ideas, so that will be your limit. Keep this card with you at all times and refer to it when you need to relax.

Here are some words you could write down: breathe; slow down; don't pace; listen; don't yell; don't glower.

You can use the card to remind yourself to breathe deeply instead of panicking; to slow down and not pace (reminders that speeding up your body is a sign that you're losing control.) The card would also remind you to listen and not yell, keeping open the lines of communication. Finally, "don't glower" reminds you not to start glaring or scowling.

Here's your space to decide what you most need on your card:

Remember: Keep your card with you at all times

Exercise 7C: Shouting Won't Make You Feel Better: Beware the Myth of Ventilation

Roger gets awfully worked up when he's angry. He does that on purpose. He says he's getting out all his feelings. He thinks it's unhealthy to stifle his anger. So, instead of trying to contain his anger, he lets it fly. He shouts, screams, throws things, and even hits people. He doesn't care if others object, either. That's their problem as far as he's concerned, not his.

How much are you like Roger? Answer yes or no.

_____ It is a good idea to yell and shout when I get mad?

_____ It is actually healthy to explode from time to time?

_____ Does it feel good to let it all out?

_____ Is it my problem if others can't handle my anger?

Roger believes in what's now called the myth of ventilation. This myth has four parts.

1. There's nothing wrong with yelling and screaming when you get angry.

2. A good explosion from time to time is actually healthy.

3. Besides, it feels good to let it all hang out once in a while.

4. It's the other person's problem if he or she can't handle your anger.

The problem with this myth is that all four arguments are flawed.

1. There is something very wrong with exploding. *Every time you explode you are teaching yourself to explode even more.* You are training yourself to lose control more and more often. Each explosion predicts another and another and another.

2. True, it's not healthy to stifle your anger. Doing this often leads to headaches and other health problems. But exploding isn't healthy, either. In fact, you may be killing yourself by getting too angry too often. Angry people on average die years earlier than calm people because of strokes, fights, and anger-related accidents.

3. Being out of control, which goes along with an anger explosion, usually feels bad, not good.

4. It's your problem, not anyone else's, if someone can't handle your anger. You're the one who's going to be avoided, punished, or ridiculed. And you're the one who will probably feel stupid and guilty after you're done exploding. It's not the world that has to adjust to you. It's you who has to adjust to the world.

The myth of ventilation has four parts. Which one do you most have to let go of? What will you think instead? _____

_____

One more thing. Exploding in anger is a luxury you cannot afford. Do you believe that? Why? _____

_____

It is important to express your feelings in moderation. See exercise 9B on the use of "I" statements for help in doing that.

Exercise 7D: Breaking the Shame-Rage Connection

Shame is the sense that there is something wrong deep inside you, something very hard or impossible to correct, as if there were a flaw in your basic character or personality.

Thoughts that often go along with the sense of shame:

- I'm no good.

- I'm not good enough.

- I'm unlovable.

- I don't belong.

- I should not exist.

Bodily sensations that often accompany the sense of shame:

- Blushing

- Feeling totally exposed

- Wanting to run

- Wanting to hide your face

- Looking down or away from others

- Paralysis—feeling frozen on the spot

And—sometimes—a tremendous urge to clobber the person or people who have triggered your feelings of shame.

Shame is a powerful emotion. It's not all bad, though. A little shame once in a while helps you fit in with others and lets you know what you need to do to feel good. But shame can be a real problem when it hits too strongly or without warning. Unexpected shame can feel like someone snuck up from behind and smacked you in the back of the head.

Here's an example:

Sarah is a thirty-year-old woman returning to school at a local college. She's worked hard for this opportunity, putting money aside from her waitressing job, so she can take software-design classes. Most of her friends and family have been really supportive. But then Sarah mentions her plans to one friend, Tess, who says, "Sarah, you're a dope. By the time you take those classes there won't be any need for more software designers. You're always behind the times."

Now Sarah is usually pretty calm and nice. But not this time. Instead, she feels herself becoming enraged. She's steaming mad. Sarah is so angry, she can barely keep from choking her friend.

"How dare you say that to me!" she yells. "I'm not a dope. You are. Besides, you'll never amount to anything because all you want to do is get drunk every night. You're stupid, too." Sarah stomps off, swearing to herself she will never talk with Tess again.

What happened?

Sarah expected praise. Instead, she was criticized. The criticism was directed at her personality ("You're a dope"), so Sarah felt disrespected and shameful. Her shame triggered feelings of rage. She attacked Tess by shaming her ("You're stupid").

The shame-rage connection occurs whenever you defend against your own feelings of shame by attacking others. The goal of a shame-rage attack is to belittle, weaken, humiliate, or even destroy the person who offended you.

Shame-rage is a little like those old Westerns in which two gunslingers square off, and one says to the other: "There's only enough room for one of us in this town, buddy." The only difference is that now they say: "There's only enough pride for one of us in this room, pal. One of us has to feel shame." And then they fight it out, using shame as their weapon as they try to kill off each other's sense of self-worth.

Here are some problems with the shame-rage connection:

- It is dangerous: people can get killed when they are fighting about shame.

- People who are oversensitive to criticism may think they are being shamed, disrespected, or embarrassed by others when nobody is doing that.

- Sometimes others accidentally say or do something that triggers another's shame. (It just makes the situation worse if you think they meant to hurt you when they didn't.)

- Shaming others when you yourself feel shame usually makes the situation worse. Problems don't get resolved by calling each other names or by attacking each other.

Sometimes people don't even realize that shame is involved ("He said something and I got mad"). The anger comes on so quickly that the person doesn't even connect it with shame. It's harder to break the shame-rage connection if you don't realize that there is one.

How often do you think your anger is connected with shame?

____ Never

____ Once in a while

____ Frequently

____ Almost always

Can you think of a time when you became really angry to defend against shame? Yes ____ No ____

What did someone say or do that triggered your feelings of shame? _____

_____

_____

How did you respond? What did you think, feel, say, and do? _____

_____

_____

_____

_____

What were the results of your actions? _____

_____

_____

_____

Breaking the Shame-Rage Connection:

First, learn all you can about shame so that you can recognize when you are feeling shame. Knowledge is a great ally in the fight against rage. Besides, shame thrives in the dark. Bringing it out into the open drains its power over you.

Second, identify your shame triggers. What could someone say to you that would really get you mad? What could they say that might trigger a shame-rage attack? What have people said in the past that did trigger a shame-rage episode?

Shame trigger 1: _____

Shame trigger 2: _____

Shame trigger 3: _____

Shame trigger 4: _____

Third, buy time when you feel the start of a shame-rage surge. These rages come on really fast, so you must be very careful not to say or do anything harmful when they first strike. You've got to say something like this to yourself: "Whoa, slow down. This must be my shame. Don't let it take control." See exercise 5A for help.

Fourth, stay respectful of others. Never respond to feeling shamed by shaming others. That will only turn a bad situation into a disaster.

Fifth, discuss the situation with the person or people who offended you. Tell the person who has said or done something that triggered your shame about what happened. People will usually apologize or explain that they didn't mean to insult you. After all, most people don't go around looking for trouble. However, don't take this step if the person who has offended you has a long history of intentionally humiliating others.

Sixth, work on your shame issues, so you become less vulnerable to shame-rage episodes. Reading helps. Therapy also helps some people. Hanging around people who like and respect you is very important.

Please review the six steps above. Will you make a commitment to follow them? _____

CHAPTER 8

Containment: Spirit

Exercise 8A: Discovering the Wounded Idealist Hiding Behind Your Sarcasm, Cynicism, and Put-downs

Frank, a twenty-one-year-old student, was a cynic. He loved to make sarcastic remarks, the kind that really cut people down. One day his friend Del invited Frank to go to a talk. The talk was on the topic of joy. Frank spent the entire hour making cynical comments like, "That's bullshit" and "What's joy got to do with anything? Life sucks and then you die." He kept a perpetual sneer on his face.

Something remarkable happened at the end of that talk, though. Del turned to Frank and said he had a question for him. "Frank," he asked, "why are you so sarcastic? What good does it do you?" Frank couldn't answer. He didn't know. He went home and thought about that question for a long time. And he still didn't know. He realized he had gradually become a cynic, attacking everything other people believed in. But he hadn't always been that way. He had once been much more optimistic and hopeful. Frank had been happier then. Much happier.

How much are you like Frank? Do you like to put people down? Do people accuse you of having fun at their expense? Is your humor too biting? Do you frequently make sarcastic remarks? Do you sneer at other people's hopes and dreams? Do people say that you sound bitter or that you have an "attitude problem"? Like Frank, are you killing off your own dreams as well as those of everybody else?

On a scale of 0 to 100, with 100 being highest, how sarcastic are you? _____

Is that where you want to be? _____

What's one of your most common sarcastic remarks? _____

_____

Why do you think you are so sarcastic? _____

_____

What good does your cynicism and sarcasm do you? _____

_____

I have a theory: *Scratch a cynic and you'll discover a wounded idealist inside.* Someone who once believed that the world is a pretty good place. Someone who had positive goals, dreams to follow, hopes for the future. But then something happened. Perhaps a single awful experience, such as a death, trauma, betrayal, or loss. Maybe a long series of disappointments—illnesses, lay offs, relationship breakdowns—that ate away at the idealist's optimism like acid on the soul. Slowly this person developed a layer of defenses around the pain, like an oyster growing a pearl. Inside the pearl are buried hopes and dreams. But on the outside is a layer of anger and bitterness. All others see is the outer layer, the defensiveness. But the hope lingers deep inside, waiting to be released.

Does this describe you? If yes, how do you know? _____

_____

If your answer is "maybe," write down why you may be a wounded idealist.

_____

_____

_____

What painful experiences have you gone through that may have contributed to your becoming more sarcastic? _____

_____

Who gets to see your hidden idealist? _____

_____

What dreams, goals, hopes, beliefs, and wants have you been hiding under that layer of cynicism? _____

_____

Are you ready to become less sarcastic and cynical? Will you make a twenty-four-hour commitment not to make any sarcastic remarks, starting now?

If yes, go for it. If no, why not? _____

_____

_____

If you make a twenty-four-hour commitment not to make any sarcastic or cynical remarks, come back to this page tomorrow and answer these questions:

- Were you able to keep your commitment? _____

- How easy or hard was it not to be cynical or sarcastic? _____

- How do you feel about yourself now? _____

  _____

- Are you willing to make another twenty-four-hour commitment? _____

- Why or why not? _____

  _____

Exercise 8B: Why Am I So Critical of Others?

- "You don't know what you're talking about."

- "Oh, Herb, you did it again. That shirt doesn't go with your tie."

- "I don't mean to criticize, but . . ."

- "You shouldn't do it that way."

- "What's wrong with you?"

Almost everybody becomes more critical when they are angry. After all, one message in anger is "I don't like what you're doing. Stop it right now."

Criticism can get out of hand, though. Already upset, you lash out at someone, saying exactly why he or she is an absolute moron. That person feels offended and counterattacks. You say things you may soon regret, but by then the damage has been done. Excessive criticism only makes a bad situation worse.

There's one more big problem with criticism. Criticism is a spiritual trap. You can get stuck there, thinking negative things about everybody and everything. You then develop a habit of criticism that keeps you from noticing the good in people. You become mean-spirited.

There are all kinds of critics. Here are a few examples.

Nitpickers. Do you frequently tell others about little things they're doing wrong? _____

Grumblers. Is nothing ever good enough for you? _____

Slammers. Do you believe in fighting hard? Do you go for the jugular, saying whatever you think will hurt the other person the most? _____

The perpetually disappointed. Is one of your favorite phrases, "I'm a little disappointed with you?" _____

Guilt-trippers. Do you not only tell people what they're doing wrong but also expect them to feel guilty about it? _____

Comparers. Do you often mention that Uncle Willie could hit the ball farther or Aunt Susie makes more money or little Ralphie gets better grades, thus destroying someone else's pride? _____

Name callers. Do you call people names like "retard," "fat slob," and "bitch" when you get angry? _____

Why are you so critical? Below are several possible reasons. Check off the ones that fit you. Being critical of others . . .

_____ Helps me feel superior/dominant.

_____ Convinces me I'm right and you're wrong.

_____ Protects me against their criticism by striking first.

_____ Helps me avoid noticing my imperfections and faults.

_____ Keeps me in control by making others feel dumb, weak, or bad.

_____ Is like what I do to myself—I'm very critical of myself.

_____ Keeps others from getting too close to me.

_____ Is my way of trying to help or protect or guide others, whether they like it or not.

_____ Feels good—I enjoy putting people down.

_____ Protects my image because what they do reflects on me.

_____ Helps me feel noticed by making people pay attention to me.

Now that you better understand why you are critical, please write your response to one more question: How might your life be changed if you quit being so critical?

_____

_____

_____

The Ultimate Challenge

Go talk with someone close to you, someone you've frequently criticized. Tell that person you've been thinking a lot about why you are so critical. Tell this person that you now realize it's a lot more about you than him or her. Show the reasons you've checked off. Be honest. You may need to apologize. You may want to promise to be far less critical in the future. Whatever you do, though, don't begin by apologizing only to end by criticizing this person even more. And don't expect the other person to promise to be less critical of you. The purpose is for you, not them, to talk openly about something you need to change.

Make yourself a list of all the people you have criticized. List them in the order that you need to talk with them.

The person I need to talk with is: _____

The second person I need to talk with is: _____

The third person I need to talk with is: _____

Do you want to become less critical of others? If so, you'll want to pay special attention to the next two exercises. First you'll need to start looking for the good in people instead of the bad. Next you'll want to substitute praise for criticism as you talk with people.

Exercise 8C: Looking for the Good in Others: A Healing Medicine

Being too critical can be dangerous to your soul. Too much criticism of others slowly kills your spirit. Fortunately, there is something you can do to become less critical. That is to focus on the good, instead of the bad, in others. Train yourself to look for the good and your spirit can heal. The most important time to see the good in others isn't when they are being perfect or when they are doing exactly what you want. It's easy to be positive then. No, the most important time to look for goodness is when you are most tempted to criticize, namely when others are saying or doing something you don't like.

Your twelve-year-old son scribbles a few lines on paper and gets ready to turn it into his teacher. You could criticize: "Son, that paper is a piece of crap. You can't hand that in." But, instead, you could look for something good: "Son, you've got a couple good ideas there, especially the one on . . ."

Your partner comes up with some possibilities for redecorating the bedroom. You could criticize: "Another stupid idea. Besides, you know we can't afford that." Or you could stay positive: "I'm glad you're thinking about this stuff. It sure doesn't hurt to talk about it."

Your boss comes through with a massive project revision. You could be negative and hostile: "That ass. Now I'll have to change everything." But what if you looked for the good, instead of the bad? Maybe you'll find something in this new plan that will actually improve the final product.

Noticing the good in people and events is a lifetime goal. It's not something you do once or twice for practice. It's something you must choose to do every day. Fortunately, though, the more you look for the good, the easier it gets. The funny thing is that the more you train yourself to look for the good, the more good you will find. It's been there all along, of course, but maybe you were too busy looking for things to criticize to notice.

Think a few minutes about the last twenty-four hours of your life. Can you name two times you let yourself see something good in the world? Write them down.

1. _____

2. _____

Now set a goal for the next twenty-four hours to notice at least three good things about the world or other people. Then write them down tomorrow.

1. _____

2. _____

3. _____

The next day, try to notice at least four good things about the world or other people. Once again write them down at the end of the day.

1. _____

2. _____

3. _____

4. _____

Keep doing this every day for at least a month. You're gradually retraining your brain to think in an entirely different way, so it will take time. But if you keep at this task you will eventually see and live in an entirely different world.

Next step: Set a goal of noticing the good in others during moments when you would otherwise only see their badness. Keep a record of those times when you could have paid attention to what they were doing wrong but instead you chose to notice something good about them.

1. I could have complained about _____

   but instead I noticed _____

2. I could have complained about _____

   but instead I noticed _____

3. I could have complained about _____

   but instead I noticed _____

4. I could have complained about _____

   but instead I noticed _____

Exercise 8D: Helpless Fury/Impotent Rage

- You just got a great job review. But, instead of a raise, you're told that they're laying you off because business is slow.

- No matter how hard you try, you simply cannot do that math assignment.

- Just when you thought you were finally getting caught up financially, the roof on your home starts to leak.

- Your boyfriend or girlfriend suddenly breaks up with you and won't return your calls.

- The judge rules that your ex-spouse gets full custody of the kids, even though you're the better parent.

- Someone you love is dying from alcoholism or drug addiction. You've tried a hundred ways to convince this person to stop, but nothing works.

Have you ever felt so angry you wanted to shake your fist at the sky? Something awful was happening to you, but there was nothing you could do about it. That's probably when you felt moments of helpless fury, or impotent rage.

Feeling this angry and helpless is like being trapped in a car that's stuck on the tracks as a speeding train approaches. You're kicking as hard as you can at the door, shouting in rage, but it refuses to open.

Here are some of the elements of helpless fury:

- Something very bad is happening or might happen.

- You desperately want to do something that will make things better, but nothing you do has any positive effect.

- You keep trying, hoping, praying. You believe that you can't give up; it's too important. You think you can't walk away.

- All the while you are becoming more and more frustrated, anxious, and depressed.

- You begin feeling absolutely helpless and hopeless.

- You get angry at anybody who doesn't help you and at people who try to help but can't.

- You get angry at the universe, at God, at fate. Life seems incredibly unfair.

- You get really angry at yourself because you cannot fix, change, or control things.

When's the last time you felt helpless fury? What about?

_____ I'm feeling that way right now about _____

_____

_____ Within the last month about _____

_____

_____ Within the last year about _____

_____

_____ Within the last few years about _____

_____

_____ A long time ago about _____

_____

_____ I never have felt helpless fury.

What can you do when you feel helpless fury?

Remember this acronym: CAP which stands for *creativity, acceptance,* and *patience.*

Creativity. Use creative problem solving. Perhaps you can think of a new way to approach this problem. One of the strongest messages in helpless fury is that what you are doing isn't working. So the first question to ask is this: Is there anything different that I could do instead of repeating the stuff that isn't effective? For example, think of the person with an alcoholic spouse. What hasn't he or she tried yet? Perhaps attending a meeting of Al-Anon might help, or perhaps seeing a counselor to arrange an intervention would be a worthwhile move.

It's easy to get stuck in bad situations, doing the same things over and over. Think of a situation in which you feel or felt helpless fury. Then answer these questions:

- What have I done so far (or what did I do) that hasn't changed the situation?

_____

_____

- Is there anything new or different I could try? _____

_____

_____

Acceptance. Another message in helpless fury is that you may be trying to do the impossible. As human beings, we are limited. We will never be totally in control of our lives. It's not always easy to accept that reality, especially when something bad is happening. But acceptance may be the only way to get through the pain.

Think of a situation in which you feel (or felt) helpless fury. Then answer these questions:

- What is (was) hardest for me to accept about the situation in which I feel (or felt) impotent rage? _____

_____

_____

- How could I even begin to accept this situation? _____

_____

_____

- What would help me accept things as they are? _____

_____

_____

- What must I do (or quit doing) to accept this painful reality? _____

_____

_____

Patience. Sometimes things change much more slowly than you wish. The back pain that has kept you from working is getting better, but oh so slowly. The kids who haven't talked with you since the divorce are only beginning to say hello on the phone. That raise you were offered is still in the works, even though it was supposed to start two months ago.

Sometimes when you feel helpless fury, you just need to be more patient. Being patient may not be your natural style, but learning patience may be the only way you can survive some situations. Again, think of a situation that makes (or made) you feel helpless.

- It is (was) hard to be patient in this situation because _____

_____

_____

- But if I don't get more patient I might _____

_____

_____

- One thing I can remind myself of that will help me be patient is _____

_____

_____

- Being patient in this situation will help or would have helped) _____

_____

_____

Remember, CAP: creativity, acceptance, patience—the three keys to handling impotent rage.

PART III

Resolution

Anger has two great values. It tells you there is something wrong and it gives you energy to do something about it. But anger is never a total answer to anything. Alone, it cannot solve your problems. Anger is merely an emotional messenger. Anger points you in a direction, but it cannot get you where you want to go all by itself.

That's where conflict-resolution comes into the picture. The goal of conflict-resolution is to settle problems. Conflict-resolution is a set of skills such as fair fighting, negotiating, and praise-giving. The more of these skills you master, the better you'll get at actually resolving conflict. The ideal conflict-resolution occurs when everyone gets everything they most want. That's not always possible, of course. But people can almost always find ways to compromise. They may not get all their hopes met, but they can get some.

Your anger will naturally dissolve when conflict-resolution works. One reason is because you won't have anything to be angry about, once an issue is resolved. Another reason is that a well-handled conflict helps you feel good about yourself and others. ("Hey, I can do this. We can do this.") Nothing builds confidence better than success.

The purpose of this last section of the workbook, then, is to provide you with a useful set of skills. You can use any one of these skills to help you deal with a particular problem. Together, they will help you handle almost any conflict.

CHAPTER 9

Resolution: Actions

Exercise 9A: Praise

- Praise (official definition): To approve or admire.

- Praise (informal definition): Saying something positive about someone else.

- Praise (when you are angry): Words that get stuck in your throat and seldom get spoken.

- Praise (for people who've been angry a long time): A lost art.

Praise is a communications skill. To get good at it, you have to quit looking for things to criticize (see exercise 8B) and start looking for the good in others (see exercise 8C). But that's not enough. Next, you have to tell people what you're noticing.

- "Hey, Bob, good meal!"

- "What a beautiful smile."

- "Thanks, Mary. You did a great job."

- "You said that just perfectly."

You may be wondering how praise helps resolve conflict. Alone, it doesn't settle anything. But praise lessens anger. It's simply hard to stay really mad at someone who mentions what they like about you. Praise lowers negativity, rigidity, and meanness. It increases good feelings both in the praise receiver and the praise giver. Praise leads to more praise and less criticism.

Four cautions:

1. Don't let those words of praise get stuck in your throat. They won't do any good until they get spoken.

2. Don't give false praise. That's when you say something you don't mean.

3. Don't expect or demand to get praised by the person you praise. That might happen, but it might not and then you'll just have another excuse to get angry.

4. Above all, don't follow any words of praise with the word *but*, as in "Jody, I liked the mashed potatoes, but they were a little soggy." Following praise with criticism is like following a kiss with a punch in the nose.

Here's a list of things to praise:

Accomplishment. "Good job." "You did it." "I'm impressed." "That's the way."

Effort. "Good try." "Keep at it." "Great start." "I appreciate the hard work."

Thinking. "Good thinking." "You figured it out." "That was a thoughtful comment."

Appearance. "Nice smile." "Beautiful hair." "You're looking great."

Morals/values. "Thanks for being honest." "You have good character." "I like the way you stand up for what you believe in."

Creativity. "You're very creative." "I like how you see things a little differently than I do." "You draw beautifully."

Concern for others. "You're generous." "You're so caring." "That was very kind of you."

Common sense. "That makes sense." "You're very practical." "You get to the root of things."

Taste. "You have a great sense of color." "You sure know what goes with what." "You've got great taste in . . ."

The kinds of praise I'm best at are: _____

_____

_____

On the other hand, I could give a lot more praise in these areas: _____

_____

_____

_____

Choosing to Praise: A Visualization

Find a comfortable place to sit, and close your eyes. Imagine yourself walking up to someone important in your life and giving them praise. Be specific in what you tell them. Mention exactly what they do that you appreciate. Then imagine that person taking in your praise, breathing deeply, smiling, thanking you, relaxing. And then notice how good you feel, the good way you feel whenever you give someone a gift they really like.

Keep going. Walk up in your imagination to another person and repeat the process. Continue. Imagine next walking up to someone with whom you haven't gotten along very well. See yourself giving that person some real praise. Feel them taking in your praise, perhaps hesitating at first, but then relaxing and believing you. Again, notice the good feelings you have when you praise others.

End with giving praise to someone you love. Imagine the positive effects on that person's self-esteem. Watch that person feeling better and better as he or she takes in your praise. And then notice that you too feel better about yourself. You're less angry and more open to the world. Finish by opening your eyes and sitting quietly for a minute or two.

Giving praise isn't hard once you decide to do it. Are you ready?

Exercise 9B: "I" Statements: Feeling and Action Versions

My friend Ed Ramsey says you catch more flies with honey than vinegar. So why then do most people keep using vinegar instead of honey in a conflict? The vinegar comes in the form of attacks, insults, threats, vague comments, and exaggerations. These behaviors only increase the likelihood that others will react defensively. Fortunately, there is a way to talk with people that is more like honey than vinegar. You'll find that people usually are much more willing to listen to you when you use "I" statements.

The purpose of an "I" statement is to help you tell someone exactly what bothers you, how their behavior affects you, and how you want them to change. "I" statements help resolve conflicts because they keep the discussion clear and specific. "I" statements also help you stay centered and self-aware during a conflict. They are the opposite of "you" statements, as in, "You did this and you did that to me."

The classic "I" statement is feelings-oriented. Here's what it looks like:

1. You tell the other person what they have done (or failed to do) that bothers you: "Joe, last night you said you'd be home by midnight but you didn't get back until three A.M."

2. You then state your feelings: "I felt scared and angry."

3. And then you tell the other person what you want: "Please call me if you are going to get home later than you told me."

The feelings-oriented "I" statement works well whenever your feelings matter to the person you're confronting. That person—perhaps your partner, parent, child, sibling, or a good friend—probably didn't do whatever he or she did to make you feel bad. This person may be quite willing to change his or her behavior after realizing its affect on you.

On the other hand, there may be situations where you're talking with someone who doesn't really care all that much about your emotional well-being: a competitor, a family member too angry to care, your boss. In this case, a more effective "I" statement will substitute an action remark in the second stage of the "I" statement for the feelings remark.

1. Other person's bothersome behavior: "Joe, you said you'd get that report to me today. But it's not here."

2. Then say how that affects you. Be specific. "Now I can't complete my cost estimate for the bid that's due tomorrow."

3. And again tell the other person exactly what you want. "I need that report by noon today."

Notice that there's no guarantee you'll get what you want in either case. But that's life. Your job is to inform the other person as clearly as possible about what you want and need.

Can you think of a situation in your life right now in which you could use an "I" statement? What is it? _____

Which form (feelings or action) would best fit the situation? _____

Why? _____

_____

_____

Your "I" Statement

1. What specifically did the other person do (or fail to do) that is bothering you?

_____

_____

2. What do you feel? (Or, how has that affected your life?) _____

_____

_____

3. What specifically do you want? _____

_____

_____

Exercise 9C: Fair Fighting

You're unhappy with your roommate, Vanessa. You think she should pay a greater share of the expenses because she's home more than you. She thinks a fifty-fifty split is fair. You're tempted to bash her with a few mean words just to hurt her. But you know that will only make the situation worse. You decide to fight fair.

Why fight fair? Fair fighting works better than unfair fighting. You stay respectful of the other person. That means the other person will probably do the same for you. Mutual respect lessens defensiveness. Less defensive people think better. And people who think better come up with better solutions to their disagreements.

Here are the basic guidelines for fair fighting. <u>Don't</u> ever:

- Make fun of others.

- Hit, push, shove, hold, threaten.

- Stand up and yell.

- Interrupt.

- Make faces.

- Attack the other person's personality.

- Call the other person names.

- Get stuck in the past.

- Run away from the issue.

- Generalize.

- Say "forget it," "tough," "who cares?", "so what?", or other dismissive phrases.

- Have to get in the last word

But you should always:

- Stick to one issue at a time.

- Sit down and talk quietly.

- Tell people what you feel.

- Listen.

- Be clear and specific.

- Make regular eye contact (but don't glare).

- Stay flexible.

- Be willing to negotiate and compromise.

- Breathe calmly, stay relaxed.

- Take responsibility for everything you say.

- Focus on solutions, not victories or defeats.

- Take time-outs as needed.

A Personalized Short List of Fair Fighting Rules

The list above is pretty long. There are too many ideas here to think about all at once. Keep the list, though. Tape it to your refrigerator door, or any place you will see it regularly.

A big list like this becomes most useful when you personalize it. You do that by selecting the things you most need to work on. Follow these steps: Circle the three or four items on the "don't" list you most need to remember. For instance, you might circle "don't make faces," "don't interrupt," and "don't get stuck in the past."

Circle the three or four items on the "you should always" list you most need to remember in a conflict. For example, "listen," "sit down and talk," and "be willing to negotiate and compromise."

Practicing Fair Fighting

Fair fighting is a skill. The more you practice, the better you get at it. So, see if you can dig up someone willing to practice with you. But don't choose a person you're really angry with. Find someone with whom you can play and have a little fun while you learn.

Pick a pretend topic to disagree about, such as which car is better to buy, the pink Cadillac or the gray Lexus; or whose mother is a better cook. It doesn't matter what topic you choose as long as it isn't a real problem between you.

Now use the items on your personalized "don't" list to have an unfair fight. Go ahead. Make faces. Interrupt. Get stuck in the past. (Stop if it quits being fun.) Meanwhile, have your partner do the same with his or her list of unfair tactics. Take a couple of minutes to fight unfair. Then discuss how that felt and what you accomplished.

Now try fighting fair. Use the three or four items from your list of "do's" as guidelines. Really listen. Sit down. Be willing to negotiate and compromise. Have your partner do the same. Take a couple of minutes to have a fair fight. Then discuss your feelings and results.

Repeat this practice a couple of times today, tomorrow, and next week. Try it with different partners. Meanwhile, fight fair in real life. That's where it matters most.

Exercise 9D: Apologies Made, Apologies Accepted

- "I'm too mad to admit I'm wrong."

- "I know I'm wrong, but I'm too proud to apologize."

- "They say they're sorry, but I refuse to accept it."

One way people stay angry and fail to end arguments is that they refuse to admit they're wrong. Another way is to refuse to apologize, even when they know they're wrong. And a third is to hang on to their anger by refusing to accept another's apology.

Why does this keep happening? Scan the list below and see if you can identify some of the reasons you have trouble admitting your mistakes, apologizing, or accepting an apology.

I have trouble apologizing or accepting an apology because:

_____ I'm so arrogant I really believe I'm always right about everything.

_____ I hate to admit to myself I'm ever in error.

_____ I hate to admit to others I said or did something wrong.

_____ I'm a very competitive person who never wants to lose even one round in a discussion.

_____ I get so mad I don't care if I'm right or wrong; I just want to attack the other person.

_____ I'm afraid people will laugh at me or ridicule me if I admit I made a mistake.

_____ I can't stand being less than perfect.

_____ I live by the motto, "Never forgive and never forget."

_____ I'd be giving up power and control if I admitted I was wrong.

_____ I want to keep fighting rather than actually solve problems.

_____ I'd feel bad, guilty, or ashamed if I admitted I screwed up.

_____ I'd rather stay mad than give up my anger at someone by accepting their apology.

_____ I've just never learned how to apologize or accept an apology.

Let's concentrate on that last choice: "I've just never learned how to apologize or accept an apology." Here's how to apologize:

1. Find a private spot for the apology. Apologies are best done privately. They're much less embarrassing without an audience.

2. Tell the person you've hurt or angered that you want to make an apology.

3. Then say as specifically as possible exactly what you did wrong. ("I should never have told you that you were stupid just because I disagreed with you" sure beats "I'm not sure why you're mad at me, but I guess maybe I did something wrong.")

4. Now apologize: "I'm very sorry I did that. I want to apologize."

5. Make a commitment to change your behavior in the future: "I promise I won't do that again."

6. Keep your promise. Think of an apology as a bridge connecting past mistakes with future good conduct. Your apology is only worth as much as your next action. For instance, if you tell someone you're sorry for insulting them and then call them names the next day, you have wasted that apology.

Don't insist or even expect the other person to accept your apology, forgive you, or also apologize to you. Apologies must come with no strings attached (no expectations). Apologies that come with expectations only lead to more arguments and bad feelings.

Do You Need to Apologize to Someone?

Who is it? _____

What did you do wrong? _____

_____

_____

How do you think that hurt him or her? _____

_____

_____

What do you need to say to them? (Review the steps described above.) _____

_____

_____

_____

Before you apologize, though, are you sure your apology will come with no strings attached (no expectations)? You're not ready to apologize if the answer is "yes."

Now do it. Make that apology before you lose your courage!

Here's How to Accept Apologies

1. Let the person say what he or she needs to say. Don't interrupt. Just listen attentively.

2. Express thanks for the apology and the commitment to new behavior (if the person has made one).

3. If you really think no apology was necessary, say so and explain why—but don't get into an argument about it. It's better to accept than reject an unnecessary apology if the apologizer is sincere.

4. Remember you are under no obligation to apologize just because someone else has said he or she was sorry. However, if you honestly believe you were partly responsible for whatever happened between the two of you, this certainly would be a good time to say so.

5. You may want to complete this business with a handshake or hug, which will help restore the relationship to normal.

When's the Last Time Someone Tried to Apologize to You?

Who was it? _____

About what? _____

How well did you follow the suggestions above?

_____ Very well

_____ Fairly well

_____ Not so well

_____ Terribly

What did you do right? _____

_____

What did you do wrong? _____

_____

What will you remember to do the next time someone tries to apologize to you?

_____

_____

_____

CHAPTER 10

Resolution: Thoughts

Exercise 10A: Nondefensive Conflict: Looking for the Grain of Truth in the Other's Viewpoint

It's practically impossible to settle arguments when you get defensive. That's when you insist that everything you say is accurate, correct, and sensible while everything the other person says is inaccurate, wrong, and ridiculous. ("I'm right and you're wrong, and that's all there is to it.")

Now you may feel just that way. It seems perfectly obvious you are right—completely right—and the other person is completely wrong. But that's your gut talking, not your mind. The fact is most of the time in an argument, neither party is *all* right or *all* wrong. Both have something to say that needs to be heard.

You need to train yourself to listen for the grain of truth in the other person's argument. You can do that by asking yourself the following questions during a disagreement: What is he or she saying that is at least partly true? What don't I want to accept that I need to take in? What am I saying that is exaggerated or partly untrue? Why am I getting defensive? What is the grain of truth in his or her viewpoint?

Notice this last question is not: "Is there a grain of truth in his or her viewpoint?" It is "What is the grain of truth in his or her viewpoint?" You must assume there is at least one grain and look for it. Otherwise you'll stay locked in an inflexible defensive stance.

Can you think of a disagreement where you got defensive? _____

_____

_____

With whom? _____

About what? _____

_____

_____

_____

What was your initial viewpoint? _____

_____

What was the other person's initial viewpoint? _____

_____

_____

How did you get defensive (What did you think, feel, say and do)? _____

_____

_____

_____

Now for the grain of truth:

As you think back, what was the other person saying that was at least partly true?

_____

_____

_____

What did you not want to accept that you needed to take in? _____

_____

_____

What were you saying that was exaggerated or at least partly untrue? _____

_____

_____

_____

Why were you getting defensive? _____

_____

_____

What was the grain of truth in his or her viewpoint? _____

_____

_____

_____

Exercise 10B: Be Willing to Compromise

The theme of exercise 4B was, "You can't always get what you want." The idea of this exercise is that you can't get *all* of what you want. But you usually can get some of what you want if you're willing to compromise.

Sometimes it's pretty easy to come up with a compromise. For instance:

You: Jenny, I want you home by ten tonight.

Jenny: Oh, please can't I stay out until twelve?

You: Tell you what. Let's split the difference. Will you agree to come home by eleven?

Jenny: Okay.

Sometimes it's not so easy to come up with a compromise.

You: Jenny, you have to stay home tonight and do your homework.

Jenny: No! I've got to go to the game. Please, please, please, please, please, please, please.

You: But you have a big test tomorrow.

Jenny: I know, but I've got to go to the game. Kenny will be there!

This one's going to take a while. But compromises are certainly possible. How about: "Well, it's only three-thirty now. If we quit arguing and you study for the next couple hours for the test, I'll let you go."

Learning to compromise is an art. It's also a skill. Finally, it's an attitude, a willingness to take the time and effort to seek out solutions that are acceptable to everybody.

Your Willingness-to-Compromise Scorecard

On the left side of the page are several mindsets that help people reach compromises. On the right are their opposites. Circle the number on the line between them where you think you usually belong.

Patient	+3 +2 +1 0 -1 -2 -3	Impatient
Flexible	+3 +2 +1 0 -1 -2 -3	Inflexible
Creative	+3 +2 +1 0 -1 -2 -3	Uncreative
Some is enough	+3 +2 +1 0 -1 -2 -3	Wants it all

Fights fair   +3 +2 +1 0 -1 -2 -3   Fights dirty

Respectful   +3 +2 +1 0 -1 -2 -3   Disrespectful during
                                                    conflict

Seeks good for all   +3 +2 +1 0 -1 -2 -3   Only cares about self

So what's your score? _____

    If your score is less than 0 in any area, you will have trouble compromising.

    If it is less than 0 overall, you have a lot of work to do.

    If it is +7 or higher, you will probably be able to reach compromises most of the time.

    The goal is to improve your score. Start with the areas below 0.

I need to improve my ability to compromise by working first on: _____

_____

_____

I could get that area up to +1 or better by: _____

_____

_____

I want to get my total score up to _____ by this date: _____

I plan to do that by remembering to _____

_____

_____

Exercise 10C: Keeping Things in Perspective

Here is a vital question to ask yourself when you are bothered by someone's behavior or ideas and you want them to change: On a scale of 1 to 10 how important is this particular issue?

10   **Life threatening.** Someone's health or safety is immediately at risk.

9   **Critical.** The situation cannot be ignored without serious damage almost certainly occurring to someone or something.

8   **Very serious.** Something pretty bad could happen unless the issue gets handled immediately.

7   **Distressing.** Something is going on that seriously violates your values and beliefs but isn't immediately dangerous.

6   **Disturbing.** You have a bad feeling about something because it might violate your values and beliefs.

5   **Troublesome.** You are bothered by the other's actions or words not because of what the other is doing but because you fear it could lead to disturbing behavior later.

4   **Displeasing.** You don't like the other's actions or words because they aren't what you would do or want them to do.

3   **Irritating.** The other's behavior or ideas are unpleasant to you but don't affect your life at all.

2   **Annoying.** It bothers you that the other person says or does things differently than you.

1   **Trivial.** The other's choices really have no effect upon you and they aren't about anything serious, either.

Here are a few situations to think about. Where would you rank each one and why?

1. Your kid sister, age sixteen, tells you she's dating a thirty-two-year-old guy.
Problem rating _____ Why? _____

2. Your partner wants to go gambling with the $3,000 you just received as a work bonus while you want to put it away for a rainy day.
Problem rating _____ Why? _____

3. Your friend decides that tonight's the night to kill the man who stole his girl-friend.
   Problem rating _____ Why? _____

4. Your boss orders you to lie to a client about the need for costly repairs.
   Problem rating _____ Why? _____

5. Your son decides to drop out of college and join a rock band.
   Problem rating _____ Why? _____

6. Your spouse likes to listen to classical music which you don't prefer.
   Problem rating _____ Why? _____

Now take a couple of situations going on right now in your life. Rate each one just like above. Caution: It's easy to rate situations too high when you're angry. Be careful not to exaggerate.

What's the problem? _____

Problem rating _____ Why? _____

What's the next problem? _____

Problem rating _____ Why? _____

Using this rating system will help you keep things in perspective. You'll probably discover that a lot of things that bother you really should be scored pretty low on the scale. In fact, they may be so low that the best thing you could do would be to ignore them entirely. Anything under about a 5 on the scale certainly isn't worth getting bent out of shape over.

The hardest decisions about what you should do come in the middle range from 5 to 8 on the scale. Should you say something or keep your mouth shut? Should you lay down the law or try to be flexible? This is the area where the skills of compromise and negotiation, the ideas mentioned in exercise 10B, are most useful.

But what if something really is critical or life-threatening? Then you have to take a stand. Compromise may not be possible in these very serious situations. Sometimes you simply have to say no.

- "No, I won't let you take the kids for a drive right now. You're drunk and I've got to protect them."

- "Boss, I just won't do it. I won't lie to our customers."

Keep things in perspective. That's the only way to resolve problems. Don't let something small become something huge.

Exercise 10D: Enough, Already! Stop Being So Stubborn

Hand someone a paintbrush when they're angry, and they'll probably paint themselves into a corner. They get into impossible situations and then sit there watching the paint drying while their relationships suffer permanent damage.

You may be an expert at painting yourself into corners. If so, you probably have a well-deserved reputation for stubbornness, as in, "No, I won't change my mind" and "I won't back down no matter what" and "I refuse to compromise. It's my way or the highway." You won't budge, no matter what.

How Stubborn Are You?

Which of these statements best describes you?

_____ I'm incredibly stubborn. Once I take a stand, I almost never let go, compromise, negotiate or change my mind. I have exceptionally strong opinions about many things.

_____ I'm very stubborn. It's hard for me to let go of things, but I can do so if I really work at it.

_____ I'm fairly stubborn. I often get stuck in inflexible positions. I'm frequently too rigid about how things should be done.

_____ I'm not very stubborn. Once in a while I get stuck holding on to an idea too long, but I'm pretty good at compromising, letting go, and changing the way I think about things.

_____ I'm not stubborn at all. I'm very flexible. I can let go of my opinions easily in order to reach a compromise or to quit fighting.

Now ask three of your closest friends or relatives whether or not they agree with you. Using the above list, ask them to rate you on a 0-to-4 scale of stubbornness, with 0 being "not stubborn at all" and 4 being "incredibly stubborn."

First person's name: _____ rates you a ____ on the stubbornness scale.

Second person's name: _____ rates you a ____ on the stubbornness scale.

Third person's name: _____ rates you a ____ on the stubbornness scale.

If your friends rated you higher on the stubbornness scale than you did, believe them. You're more stubborn than you think.

Do you need to become less stubborn? The answer should be "yes" whenever you find that you've painted yourself into a corner, fighting about things when you really just want to get on with your life.

But how can you become less stubborn? By changing some of your thoughts, namely the ones that keep you from compromising or letting go.

You can change "Compromising means I have to give in" to "Compromising means everybody has to give in" or to "Compromising means getting something done."

Now it's your turn . . .

Change "I never change my opinions" to _____

_____

Change "I'm just a stubborn person" to _____

_____

Change "I'm too proud to back down" to _____

_____

Change "Making my point is more important than anything else" to _____

_____

Change "I won't let go of my ideas no matter what" to _____

_____

Change "Negotiation is an act of weakness" to _____

_____

Change "When I get angry, I'm like a stubborn mule" to _____

_____

Change "I don't think of myself as being very flexible" to _____

_____

Change "In the past I haven't been able to let go" to _____

_____

CHAPTER 11

Resolution: Feelings

Exercise 11A: Understanding the Other Person's Feelings

It's easy to become self-centered when you start getting angry about something. Actually, "self-absorbed" might be a better word. You're so upset that all you notice is what's going on in your own body and mind. At that point the other person becomes an obstacle, a problem, a thing, a monster, an enemy, someone you despise. You forget that he or she is a human being with feelings.

Two questions will help you get your focus off yourself and back onto the other person: "I wonder what he/she is feeling right now?" and "I wonder what is really important to him/her right now?"

Put these together with some real caring for the other person and you have what is called *empathy*. Research has shown that empathy lessens anger. The person who cares about others and takes the time to find out what they feel and what is important to them is simply going to get less angry than someone whose mantra in life is, "Who cares about them? All I care about is myself."

Empathy is a skill. You can always get better at it. The challenge, though, is to stay empathic even when you are upset.

Empathy Practice

Select someone important to you with whom you have gotten into a disagreement lately.

What was the disagreement about? _____

_____

_____

_____

What did you want? _____

_____

_____

_____

What do you think the other person wanted? _____

_____

_____

_____

What do you think he or she was feeling? _____

_____

_____

What do you think was really important to you in this situation? _____

_____

_____

Did you ask what was important to the other person? _____

What do you think was really important to the other person? _____

_____

_____

_____

    If you can't honestly answer the questions about what the other person felt and what mattered to them, now is the time to find out. Go to him or her and ask. Just make sure you really listen to the answers.

    Make a commitment to ask three people today at least one of these two questions: "What are your feelings about this?" and "What's important to you about this?" Later, fill in the blanks below.

Who was the first person? _____

What did you ask about? _____

_____

_____

What did he or she say? _____

_____

_____

_____

Who was the second person? _____

What did you ask about? _____

_____

_____

What did he or she say? _____

_____

_____

_____

Who was the third person? _____

What did you ask about? _____

_____

_____

What did he or she say? _____

_____

_____

_____

It's important to keep practicing this skill. Remember that empathy lessens anger and helps you solve disagreements.

Exercise 11B: Checking in with Yourself to Prevent Sabotage

Have you ever almost settled a conflict only to hear yourself say those ominous words, "Yeah, but . . ."? And then everything went nuts, you both started in on each other again, and what seemed done rapidly became undone.

Why would you do that? Perhaps you still had some unfinished emotional concerns. For instance, you may have still felt:

Anger. You were trying to be reasonable but you were still mad about something.

Shame. You still felt disrespected, put down, or diminished by the other person.

Fear. Something was frightening you that hadn't been resolved.

Guilt. Nothing nags at a person more than leftover guilt, and guilt often leads to resentment of the person who "makes" you feel guilty.

Loneliness. You may have felt left out, abandoned, isolated, betrayed, or disconnected from the other person and in need of reconnecting.

These unfinished feelings are like emotional guerrilla fighters who haven't been told the war is over. They're still out there in the woods fighting. These emotional warriors are particularly good at sabotage. Their specialty is demolitions and what they blow up are the bridges of interpersonal communication and conflict-resolution. You've got to get those emotional soldiers out of the jungle before their sabotage restarts the whole war again. The way to do so is by checking your gut reaction: "Okay. We're just about done here. But before I agree to anything final, I need to ask myself a few questions."

Emotional Checklist

Do I still have any feelings I haven't talked about? If yes, what are they?

____ anger ____ shame ____ guilt ____ fear ____ loneliness ____ hurt

____ jealousy ____ disgust ____ worry ____ sadness ____ envy

____ resentment ____ other: _____

Do I have feelings I have mentioned, but still don't feel right about?

If yes, what are they? _____

Why am I holding back? _____

What good might happen if I were more emotionally honest right now? _____

_____

_____

How will I sabotage any agreements we make if I don't deal with these feelings?

_____

_____

The goal of any conflict is resolution. That includes emotional resolution. Don't quit talking until you achieve that.

Exercise 11C: Letting Go of Your Anger

You were angry with your partner. You could feel your body tensing up as your "fight or flight" reaction was triggered. But you finally settled your differences. It's over. So why do you still feel bad? One possibility, discussed in exercise 11B, is that you still have some unfinished emotional concerns. But there is another reason to consider.

The human body isn't a machine. You can't just turn off your emotions because a conflict has ended. Think of all the times you left a powerful movie still crying or sad, or those times after you've made love or had a wonderful talk when the feeling of happiness lingers. Anger, too, produces lasting sensations as your body slowly returns to normal.

Which of these sensations and reactions do you experience at the end of a conflict?

_____ Relief

_____ Irritability

_____ Fatigue/Exhaustion

_____ Nervousness

_____ Feel sick all over

_____ Headache

_____ Backache

_____ Stomachache

_____ Depression

_____ Oversensitivity

_____ Jumpiness

_____ Need for physical reassurance (hugs, holding)

_____ Need to get busy/do something

_____ Need for verbal reassurance ("I love you," etc.)

_____ Urge to eat, drink, etc.

_____ Need to be alone

_____ Need to be with people

_____ Self-destructive/suicidal

There's nothing wrong with these reactions. They are the normal costs of having a conflict. But you do need to pay attention to them. It's important to take care of your body and mind after a conflict. Don't just try to go on as if nothing has happened. Instead, take some time to heal. Think of this time like the cooling-down period that athletes take after doing strenuous exercise.

For the first thirty minutes after a conflict, I:

- Often feel _____

- Most need to _____

- Need to be careful not to _____

Over the next couple of hours, I:

- Often feel _____

- Most need to _____

- Need to be careful not to _____

For the next twenty-four hours, I:

- Often feel _____

- Most need to _____

- Need to be careful not to _____

It's a good idea to share your plan with others. They may have some helpful suggestions. They, too, may need to design their own cooling-down plans.

Exercise 11D: The Secret Attraction of Anger

Every couple of weeks Lee promises once again that he's going to change his ways and quit losing his temper so often. He tells himself he'll quit being so stubborn and actually resolve a few of his disagreements with others. But time after time he gets angry about something, blows his top, and adamantly refuses to stop arguing. He doesn't change his behavior because he really doesn't want to change. And he doesn't want to change because he has a secret.

Here's Lee's secret: He really likes the strong feelings that he gets when he blows up. That adrenaline rush turns him on. It's so intense that Lee feels almost like he's tripping on speed or cocaine. In fact, the analogy with drug-taking isn't far off. Sometimes Lee thinks he's practically addicted to his anger.

This hidden need for excitement is one big reason people fail to resolve their disagreements. Lee knows you're supposed to feel bad when you lose control of your temper. That's why he's never told anyone about what happens to him when he gets mad. He figures he's probably the only person in the world who actually gets off on anger. But perhaps he's not. Maybe you, too, like those extreme sensations that ride along with strong anger.

Excitatory Anger Checklist

Answer "yes" or "no."

1. Do you ever look for reasons to get angry? ____

2. When you're bored, do you think about getting into a fight? ____

3. Does "having a good fight" have a real appeal to you? ____

4. Do you sometimes feel really good when you are right in the middle of an argument? ____

5. Are you getting angry more often than you used to? ____

6. When you get mad, is your anger more intense than before? ____

7. To feel satisfied, do you have to get angrier now than you did in the past? ____

8. Does getting angry help you feel less anxious? ____

9. Do you feel better when you're angry? ____

10. Does getting really angry about small things seem almost irresistible to you at times? ____

11. Do you feel bad after an anger high: guilty, ashamed, depressed? ____

12. Do you later forget the things you said or did when you were very angry? ____

13. Does getting angry give you a feeling of being strong, alive, or powerful? ____

Scorecard:

"Yes" on 0–2 items: You seldom if ever get high on your anger.

"Yes" on 3–5 items: Seeking excitement probably is one of the reasons you get angry.

"Yes" on 6–8 items: You definitely get a lot of excitement from your anger.

"Yes" on 9-13 items: The thrill of getting angry is a big reason you get angry so often.

So what's the big deal? Why shouldn't I get high on anger? Here are a few good reasons:

1. You look pretty foolish yelling and screaming about stuff that really isn't important just so you have an excuse to get mad.

2. Other people get really bored with this game. They don't like playing "let's all get angry," and eventually they may leave.

3. Anger is a signal that something is wrong. It's supposed to lead to problem solving, not endless arguing. Your need for "action" makes it impossible to resolve issues or to quit fighting.

4. You can easily lose control of your anger when you use it to get high. That's when arguments become physical and dangerous.

5. Needing to get high on anger is like needing to get high on drugs. You may be becoming "addicted" to your anger, unable to control or stop it.

Eight Ways to Challenge Excitatory Anger

1. You could make a commitment to quit getting high on anger.

2. You could choose to stay calm even in situations when others get agitated or angry.

3. You could practice the art of moderation by not letting yourself get bent out of shape about anything.

4. You could find new ways to get high that don't involve anger (or drugs) such as body building, parachuting, or running.

5. You could learn better ways to disagree with people, such as negotiating and compromising, that don't involve getting into fights.

6. You could see a physician to make sure you're not depressed (because people who are depressed sometimes become thrill-seekers in an attempt to make themselves feel more alive).

7. You could tell others your secret—that you get high on anger—so they won't get sucked into helping you get high that way.

8. You could even take the equivalent of the Alcoholics Anonymous "First Step" by admitting that "I have become powerless over my anger and my life has become unmanageable."

Take a good look at those eight possibilities. Then pick the three that are most important for you to do and write them down in the spaces below:

1. _____

2. _____

3. _____

Now for a more specific plan. The next time I begin to feel an urge to get high on anger, I will:

- Remember _____

- I will not let myself _____

- Instead I will _____

CHAPTER 12

Resolution: Spirit

Exercise 12A: Looking for God in Yourself and Others

Anger is a defensive emotion. Your anger may have turned you away from something you need, namely your religion or your spirituality. You may have become angry at God and your religion, believing they have failed to help or protect you when you most needed them. But now may be a good time to consider reinvesting in religion or spirituality. That's because your religious and spiritual practices can help you greatly at times when you are angry or in conflict with others. Religion and spirituality can be a source of healing, comfort, and reconciliation.

Exercise 8C was about looking for the good in others. But there's something more you can also do that will help you be less angry. That is to look for God in others. As Quakers say, "There is that of God in everyone." The tricky part is to find it, especially when you are in conflict with another person.

What does the statement, "There is that of God in everyone," mean to you? How does that statement relate to your anger?

Here are some ways that religion and spirituality might help you deal better with your anger and conflict. Check off the ones that matter most to you.

_____ Having faith helps me believe things will turn out for the best.

_____ God forgives, so I can too.

_____ God loves everyone, so I can too.

_____ When I can feel the godliness of another, I see past our differences to what we have in common.

_____ It's easier to quit trying to control others when I remember to "let go and let God."

_____ I feel less bitter or hostile when I sense God in everyone.

_____ If there is "that of God in everyone," there must be that of God in me. Knowing that helps me forgive myself as well as others.

_____ It's easier to look for the good in people when I also look for God in them.

_____ I sometimes pray for help letting go of my anger.

_____ I seek help from religious books or leaders when I'm angry.

_____ Letting go of my anger helps me feel better spiritually—more in touch with God, my higher power, or something greater than myself.

Are you interested in making a plan to include religion and spirituality in your personal anger management package? If so, write it down here. I will pursue my religion/spirituality in the following ways:

- I will attend church/synagogue.

  Where? _____

  How often? _____

- The readings I will do are: _____

  _____

  _____

- The people I need to talk with are: _____

  _____

  _____

- When I get angry or into a conflict, I will remember _____

  _____

  _____

- Other commitments I need to make in this area are: _____

  _____

  _____

Exercise 12B: Forgiving Those Who Have Harmed You

Question: What anger is the hardest to let go of?
Answer: One that has turned into a resentment.

Question: How do resentments develop?
Answer: First someone says or does something that hurts you. You can't get it out of your mind. Your anger hardens in your mind like concrete on a sidewalk. You stay mad at the person who harmed you for days, weeks, months, even years.

Question: What eventually happens to these resentments?
Answer: They turn into hate. That means you despise the people who harmed you. You want them to suffer. You spend time fantasizing acts of vengeance against them. You want everybody else to dislike the people you hate as much as you do.

Question: What happens to people who don't let go of their resentments?
Answer: They usually become bitter. They feel trapped inside their own rage. They often do things they regret as they try to get even with those who harmed them.

Question: Why is it so hard to give up a resentment?
Answer:

1. Because then you'd have to get on with your life instead of staying stuck in the past.

2. Because you might have to accept the idea that some injustices will never get settled to your satisfaction.

3. Because then you'd have to accept full responsibility for your unhappiness instead of blaming others.

Last question: How do you get rid of resentments?
Answer: By forgiving those who have harmed you.

Are you interested in letting go of one or more of your resentments? If so, you can begin by completing the following exercise. First, select a resentment you need to let go of.

Whom do you resent? _____

Why? _____

_____

When did this all happen? _____

_____

How were you harmed? _____

_____

Now take a look at how your continuing resentment is hurting you.

How much of your time has your resentment stolen?

Today? _____

This week? _____

This month? _____

What do you say or do that only keeps you resentful? _____

_____

_____

What thoughts do you have that keep stirring you up? _____

_____

_____

How does your resentment harm or limit others? Your resentment of your brother, for instance, may keep your children from getting to know their uncle. _____

_____

_____

If you weren't so resentful, how would your life be different? _____

_____

_____

Now for the action stage. Here are personal commitments that are part of the forgiveness process. Check off those you are ready for.

_____ I'm ready to make a conscious choice to forgive someone.

_____ I'm willing to rip up old debts. In other words, I won't expect an apology, financial repayment, an "I love you," or anything else from him or her. The person I've resented no longer owes me anything.

_____ I will no longer blame this person for my misery. Instead, I will fully accept responsibility for my own pain and pleasure.

_____ I will no longer do anything to this person in the name of revenge or getting even.

_____ I will immediately quit bad-mouthing this person to others.

_____ I will start treating this person (if he or she is still in my life) with the same amount of respect and courtesy I give others. That doesn't mean I will let myself be mistreated, though.

_____ I will quit wishing or praying for bad things to happen to this person. Instead, I will begin wishing or praying for this person to find contentment and peace.

_____ I will get out of the past and put my energy into the present and future.

You may honestly realize that right now you can't make one or more of these commitments. That's okay. Forgiving is usually a gradual process. It doesn't take place overnight. The goal is to keep moving toward each of these commitments. For instance, today you may be only 10 percent of the way toward not blaming someone for your misery. But perhaps you can be 20 percent of the way by next week. If so, you're certainly doing something good and important.

There's one more thing you need to do to really begin the forgiving process. You need to write down your feelings in the form of a letter to the person or people you have resented. Here's one format you can use:

Dear _____ ,

I have been resentful of you for [how long] _____ .

I have held a grudge against you because [name specific events]

_____

_____ .

I know that holding on to that resentment has hurt you [how?]

_____

_____ .

It has hurt me [how] _____

_____ .

And it has also hurt [who else has it hurt and how?] _____

_____ .

Now I'm ready to quit resenting you because [why] _____

_____

_____

I forgive you and ask nothing in return. I will no longer expect you to [what?]

_____

Sincerely,

This is your letter, so write it in your own words and style. Just be sure to include the main ingredients expressed above.

If, after you're done, you think you may want to mail it to the person you've forgiven, take a couple days to let it rest. Show it to someone you trust and ask for comments. Reread your letter to make sure you're not asking or expecting anything from the other person. Be prepared for no response or a negative reaction. Above all, don't send this letter unless you are fully prepared to act in a non-hating manner toward this person.

Exercise 12C: Turning Anger into Advocacy: Fighting Injustice Intelligently

Anger has two main uses:

1. Anger tells you something is seriously wrong in a situation.

2. Anger gives you the energy to do something about it.

Anger Tells You Something Is Seriously Wrong

Usually what is wrong is something immediate and personal. Someone is saying or doing something right now (or very recently) that negatively affects your life. For example, your partner comes home with a $2,000 lampshade when you have exactly $500 in the bank.

Perhaps, though, the anger you feel is different. It's not about anything happening to you right now. Instead, you're angry because of some major problem in the world. You strongly believe that people are treating others badly. You feel that people are suffering from a terrible injustice.

Here are a few examples:

- A woman who was sexually abused as a child reads over and over again about other boys and girls suffering the same fate. Each time she reads another story she becomes irate. She keeps asking herself one question: "Why doesn't someone protect these children?"

- A teenage boy from a wealthy background plans to enter college next year to study law. One day he visits an inner-city friend and realizes that some kids his age go to bed hungry every night. He goes home angry about the unfairness of a world in which some people have everything they want and others have nothing.

- A man watches the woods around his state being clear-cut and begins to cry in frustration and anger.

- A couple frequently drives past an abortion clinic. They believe strongly in the right to life but have done nothing in the past to fight for that belief. But today they turn to each other and agree, "There's got to be something we can do."

- Another couple driving by that same clinic sees protesters gathered outside it urging pregnant women to stay away. "Those people have no business telling others what to do," one says to the other in obvious anger. "Someone should stick up for the right of each woman to make her own choices."

These five scenes have one thing in common. The people in them each have become angry about a perceived injustice. It seems clear to them that people are disregarding the rights of other individuals, the environment, or some basic principle. These people are not in any personal danger. They aren't angry for themselves. But they are angry, though, very angry. The anger they feel is called *outrage* or *moral anger*.

- Do you ever get angry like this? _____

- What about? _____

_____

Anger Gives You the Energy to Do Something

So something is wrong and you're angry about it. But what can you do? Shaking your fist at the sky won't help. Nor will screaming your head off to everybody and anybody who will listen. Worst of all, you'll do damage to your cause if you foolishly attack others verbally or physically. You have to be careful not to waste or misuse this strong anger you're feeling. You have to use your head.

Let's go back to the examples above. Here's one activity each of these concerned individuals could undertake:

- The previously abused woman could form a citizen's committee devoted to passing laws that better protect children from abuse.

- The teenage boy could start a "food for the hungry" kitchen. He could also decide to go to college, just as he planned, but to take courses that will prepare him for a career as an advocate for the poor.

- The outraged environmentalist could help a group buy up forest land and turn it into a public preserve.

- The couple who want to fight for the right to life could contribute to or even form an adoption agency that would give pregnant women an alternative to abortion.

- The couple who want to protect a woman's right to choose could organize a fund-raising group to support their local clinic. They could offer to speak out publicly in favor of their beliefs.

There is a name for these activities: advocacy. Here are some tips to help you advocate well for the causes you believe in:

- You should know what you are fighting for (what you believe in), not just what you are fighting against. Example: "I want all children to have access to computers because I believe everyone should start life as equals."

- Your goal should be to help others understand what good will come for them from supporting your beliefs. Example: Some African and South American communities have quit illegally poaching endangered animals because they get more income from eco-tourism.

- The methods you choose to fight for your beliefs should be strong, visible, and concrete, without trampling the rights or safety of others. Example: People who participate in "Women's Take Back the Night" rallies are advocating for a woman's right to be safe, but they aren't attacking men in the process.

- You should ask yourself, "Is this really going to do any good?" before you decide to take action. If the answer is "yes" then proceed. If the answer is "no" then change your plans. If your answer is "maybe," then take some time to think it over before jumping in. Example: An advocate for increasing literacy may decide that serving on a committee is less useful and rewarding than volunteering to teach someone how to read.

- Finally, you must be able to separate your personal issues from the more general concerns you are fighting for. That means you need to be very careful if you are advocating about something that has strongly affected your life. Example: A woman who was sexually abused as a child may make a valuable advocate against child abuse, so long as she remembers that everybody is different and that each person experiences abuse differently. She can't just say, "I know exactly how you feel," because she doesn't know that at all.

Go back to the section above in which you described what you get outraged about. Now is the time for planning. What could you do to fight for what you believe in?

_____

_____

_____

Check your ideas against the five tips above:

Can you write exactly what you are fighting for? _____

_____

_____

What good will there be for others if they agree with your position? _____

_____

_____

_____

How will you be able to take visible action without trampling the rights of others?

_____

_____

_____

What good will come from the action you're thinking of taking? _____

_____

_____

_____

Have you been able to separate your personal issues from your goal of helping others? If so, how?

_____

_____

_____

Exercise 12D: The Final Line: Doing More Good Than Harm

Have you ever been asked the deathbed question, "What would you like to have written on your gravestone after you die?" Probably not: "He was a bully and a grouch" or "She was so mean nobody liked her." But perhaps the worst message of all would be this: "You did more harm than good."

You can do far more good than harm in this world. And you will, if you stay in control of your anger. But remember that every hostile thought, every angry action, and every long held resentment damages someone. Perhaps you think that you are the only person hurt by your anger, especially when you don't tell people what's bothering you. But that's not necessarily true. Your anger creates a negative atmosphere that affects everybody around you. Think of your anger, expressed or unexpressed, as a burst of energy much like a sound wave. That wave may be too subtle to feel or hear, but it is there, affecting everybody at some level of consciousness.

Take a few minutes now to picture in your mind the people you most love and respect. They may also be the ones that you've been angry with most often. They have been harmed by your anger. But not today. Instead, imagine them all sitting together as you give each person a gift. These presents aren't material objects like bikes and rings, though. They are the positive, non-angry ways that you will treat them in the future.

Here are a few of the gifts you might offer:

____ Kindness		____ Understanding
____ Love		____ Calmness
____ Acceptance		____ Respect
____ Appreciation		____ Openness
____ Caring		____ Trust
____ Listening		____ Forgiveness
____ Involvement		____ Patience
____ Quiet		____ Space
____ Praise		____ Honesty
____ Help		____ Joy
____ Playfulness		____ Hope/Optimism
____ Attention		____ Other Feelings

Are you ready? This is the time to distribute your gifts. The only rule is that you can only give each gift one time. No two people can receive the same gift.

My gift for _____ is _____

    That's because _____

My gift for _____ is _____

    That's because _____

My gift for _____ is _____

    That's because _____

Now that you've given these wonderful gifts today, just remember one thing: Don't take them back tomorrow.

Afterword

You've now completed forty-eight exercises on anger management. Sixteen dealt with how to prevent useless conflict and unnecessary anger. Sixteen more were about containing your anger so you don't lose control. And the goal of the last sixteen was to help you learn better how to take effective action when you get angry. Those same forty-eight exercises were divided into four main areas for change: your angry actions, thoughts, feelings, and spirit.

By now you have accumulated a number of anger-management skills. The only question is how often and how well you will use them. Only you know the answer to that question.

Please remember to review these exercises frequently. You might discover that the ones most important to you now will be less so in a few months. Meanwhile, others may emerge as very useful in the near future.

My hope for you is more than that you won't get angry too often or too strongly. My hope is that you will live a good life, one in which anger has a place but doesn't dominate you. If your life is a bus, then this is the time for you to kick anger out of the driver's seat and take over the steering wheel. That being the case, I wish you a safe and interesting journey.

Some Other
New Harbinger Titles

The End of-life Handbook, Item 5112 $15.95

The Mindfulness and Acceptance Workbook for Anxiety, Item 4993 $21.95

A Cancer Patient's Guide to Overcoming Depression and Anxiety, Item 5044 $19.95

Handbook of Clinical Psychopharmacology for Therapists, 5th edition, Item 5358 $55.95

Disarming the Narcissist, Item 5198 $14.95

The ABCs of Human Behavior, Item 5389 $49.95

Rage, Item 4627 $14.95

10 Simple Solutions to Chronic Pain, Item 4825 $12.95

The Estrogen-Depression Connection, Item 4832 $16.95

Helping Your Socially Vulnerable Child, Item 4580 $15.95

Life Planning for Adults with Developmental Disabilities, Item 4511 $19.95

Overcoming Fear of Heights, Item 4566 $14.95

Acceptance & Commitment Therapy for the Treatment of Post-Traumatic Stress Disorder & Trauma-Related Problems, Item 4726 $58.95

But I Didn't Mean That!, Item 4887 $14.95

Calming Your Anxious Mind, 2nd edition, Item 4870 $14.95

10 Simple Solutions for Building Self-Esteem, Item 4955 $12.95

The Dialectical Behavior Therapy Skills Workbook, Item 5136 $21.95

The Family Intervention Guide to Mental Illness, Item 5068 $17.95

Finding Life Beyond Trauma, Item 4979 $19.95

Five Good Minutes at Work, Item 4900 $14.95

It's So Hard to Love You, Item 4962 $14.95

Energy Tapping for Trauma, Item 5013 $17.95

Thoughts & Feelings, 3rd edition, Item 5105 $19.95

Transforming Depression, Item 4917 $12.95

Helping A Child with Nonverbal Learning Disorder, 2nd edition, Item 5266 $15.95

Leave Your Mind Behind, Item 5341 $14.95

Learning ACT, Item 4986 $44.95

ACT for Depression, Item 5099 $42.95

Integrative Treatment for Adult ADHD, Item 5211 $49.95

Freeing the Angry Mind, Item 4380 $14.95

Living Beyond Your Pain, Item 4097 $19.95

Transforming Anxiety, Item 4445 $12.95

Integrative Treatment for Borderline Personality Disorder, Item 4461 $24.95

Depressed and Anxious, Item 3635 $19.95

Is He Depressed or What?, Item 4240 $15.95

Cognitive Therapy for Obsessive-Compulsive Disorder, Item 4291 $39.95

Child and Adolescent Psychopharmacology Made Simple, Item 4356 $14.95

Call **toll free, 1-800-748-6273,** or log on to our online bookstore at **www.newharbinger.com** to order. Have your Visa or Mastercard number ready. Or send a check for the titles you want to New Harbinger Publications, Inc., 5674 Shattuck Ave., Oakland, CA 94609. Include $4.50 for the first book and 75¢ for each additional book, to cover shipping and handling. (California residents please include appropriate sales tax.) Allow two to five weeks for delivery.

Prices subject to change without notice.